DATE DUE

NON-MERCHANDISE TRANSACTIONS BETWEEN CANADA AND THE UNITED STATES

by John W. Popkin

CANADIAN-AMERICAN COMMITTEE

sponsored by

National Planning Association (U. S. A.)
Private Planning Association of Canada

Reports on
Canada-United States Relations

Library of Congress Catalogue Number: 63-18003

June 1963, $1.50

Quotation with appropriate credit
is permissible

National Planning Association and
Private Planning Association of Canada, 1963

Printed in Canada

 32

ii

Contents

Tables

iv

Charts

The Canadian-American Committee

The Canadian-American Committee was established in 1957 to study problems arising from growing interdependence between Canada and the United States. With approximately equal representation from coast to coast in the two countries, its 60 members are business, labor, agricultural, and professional leaders. The Committee is sponsored by two nonprofit research organizations—the National Planning Association in the United States and the Private Planning Association of Canada.

The Committee believes that good relations between Canada and the United States are essential for the future prosperity, and perhaps even the survival, of both countries. It is therefore seeking not only to encourage a better understanding of the problems which have arisen and may arise, but also to develop solutions for such problems which are in the common interest of both countries. The Committee is taking a North American approach in its search for constructive programs.

The Committee is sponsoring a series of objective research studies on various aspects of Canadian-American relations. These are being undertaken by qualified experts in both countries and, with the Committee's approval, will be published. On the basis of these factual studies and of discussions at its meetings, the Committee also issues policy statements signed by its members. Such statements are directed at increasing public understanding of the attitudes, policies, and actions which the Committee believes would best serve the mutual interests of the peoples of both countries.

The Canadian-American Committee is a unique organization, both in terms of its broadly diversified membership and in terms of its blending of factual studies and policy conclusions on Canadian-American relations. It meets twice a year, once in Canada and once in the United States. Its work is jointly financed by funds contributed from private sources in the United States and Canada and by foundation grants.

Offices on behalf of the Committee are maintained at 1606 New Hampshire Avenue, N.W., Washington 9, D.C., and at 712 Sun Life Building, Montreal, Quebec. John Miller (Assistant Chairman and Executive Secretary of NPA) serves as Secretary of the Committee, and Arthur J. R. Smith (Secretary of PPAC) is Director of Research.

R. Douglas Stuart

Robert M. Fowler

Co-chairmen of the Committee

vii

Statement
by the Canadian-American Committee on Non-merchandise Transactions Between Canada and the United States

Trade between Canada and the United States is substantially greater than that between any other two countries, and the growth in this trade over the years (both absolutely and as a proportion of total trade of each country) has contributed much to the dynamic economic development of each. But analyses of Canadian-American trade have almost invariably dealt exclusively with merchandise trade, and the rapid growth in non-merchandise transactions between the two countries has not received the careful attention which it has warranted. Moreover, the need for such clarification of non-merchandise transactions has increased greatly as a result of the rapidly increasing imbalance in such transactions. This imbalance now occupies a very prominent position in the balance of payments between Canada and the United States.

It has been inevitable that much of the work of the Canadian-American Committee has been devoted to the subject of trade across the International Boundary. Almost all of our previously published reports and policy statements have, in varying degrees, discussed such trade. And four earlier reports have dealt especially with this subject—*The Growth and Changing Composition of Trade Between Canada and the United States; Barriers to Trade Between Canada and the United States; Changes in Trade Restrictions Between Canada and the United States;* and *The U.S. Trade Expansion Act of 1962: How Will it Affect Canadian-American Trade?* The following report is therefore the fifth in this series of studies dealing specifically with trading problems. Moreover, it specifically complements the first report listed above, which deals only with merchandise trade.

In the light of the growing importance of non-merchandise trade between Canada and the United States, and the absence of careful appraisals of the forces which have contributed to important changes in such trade over the past decade, we authorized the preparation of the following study. We believe that this study will make a significant contribution to a better understanding of such transactions—particularly in the case of some of the important types of such transactions: tourist and travel expenditures; interest and dividend payments; freight and shipping expenditures; and business services and other transactions.

This is essentially a factual and descriptive study. It has not been intended to develop policy conclusions. Studies on other aspects of Canadian-American trading relations are in the course of preparation.

The Committee has been fortunate in obtaining the services of Mr. John W. Popkin, Economist of the Sun Life Assurance Company of Canada, to undertake this study. He has been assisted by Mr. Richard Setten, also of the Sun Life Assurance Company of Canada, and has had the benefit of considerable help and advice from experts in both countries, especially from experts in this field in Ottawa.

Members of the Canadian-American Committee
Signing the Statement

Co-Chairmen

ROBERT M. FOWLER
President, Canadian Pulp & Paper Association

R. DOUGLAS STUART
Director, The Quaker Oats Company

Members

WILLIAM L. BATT
Delray Beach, Fla.

T. N. BEAUPRÉ
President, British Columbia Forest Products Limited

J. A. BEIRNE
President, Communications Workers of America, AFL-CIO

RALPH P. BELL
Honorary Director, Bank of Nova Scotia

L. J. BELNAP
Chairman, Consolidated Paper Corporation, Ltd.

HAROLD BOESCHENSTEIN
President, Owens-Corning Fiberglas Corporation

GEORGE BURT
Director, Region No. 7, United Automobile, Aircraft, and Agricultural Implement Workers of America, AFL-CIO-CLC

EARL L. BUTZ
Dean, School of Agriculture, Purdue University

MARCEL FARIBAULT
President and General Manager, General Trust of Canada

HAROLD S. FOLEY
Vancouver, B.C.

DONALD GORDON
Chairman and President, Canadian National Railways

H. H. HANNAM
President and Managing Director, The Canadian Federation of Agriculture

F. PEAVEY HEFFELFINGER
Chairman of the Board, F. H. Peavey & Company

CHARLES L. HUSTON, JR.
President, Lukens Steel Company

CURTIS M. HUTCHINS
President, St. Croix Paper Company

CLAUDE JODOIN
President, Canadian Labour Congress

VERNON E. JOHNSON
Chairman of the Board, Canadian International Paper Company

JOSEPH D. KEENAN
International Secretary, International Brotherhood of Electrical Workers, AFL-CIO

W. S. KIRKPATRICK
President, The Consolidated Mining & Smelting Company of Canada Limited

R. A. LAIDLAW
Secretary and Director, R. Laidlaw Lumber Company, Ltd.

MAURICE LAMONTAGNE
Ottawa, Ont.

HERBERT H. LANK
President, Du Pont of Canada Limited

x

1
Introduction

Scope and Aim of the Study

Canada has experienced a deficit in its balance of international payments on current account in each of the past ten years. With one exception—1956—non-merchandise transactions have been the major contributor to the over-all deficit, and in 1961 and 1962 accounted for all of it. Non-merchandise transactions have grown enormously in importance over this period and have now come to occupy a very large role, both in Canada's over-all payments position and in the flow of payments between Canada and the United States. In spite of this, most analysis and discussion of Canada's current-account balance of payments continues to deal with past and prospective trends in merchandise transactions. There are several reasons for this apparent anomaly.

- The export of goods is a vitally important activity for a large segment of Canadian industry and the volume of such trade is quite sensitive even to small changes in general economic activity. Changes in merchandise trade are reported monthly and published figures are detailed and widely publicized. On the other hand, non-merchandise transactions consist of a wide variety of financial payments and services, which are important in the aggregate, but many of which are individually small and relatively unimportant.

1

- There is a general impression that non-merchandise transactions, unlike merchandise trade, arise from a multitudinous number of private decisions, reached in a pragmatic and uninhibited manner, and largely insulated from governmental control or influence. In fact, however, government regulations and policies do have an important bearing on trends in non-merchandise transactions. Examples are: the effect of the discount Canadian dollar; reductions in Canadian travelers' duty free allowable purchases on Canada's balance of payments on travel account; government policy with respect to loans and official contributions to other countries; and the effect on interest payments and receipts of changes in monetary policy and taxes that affect the international flow of capital funds. Conversely, trends in merchandise trade are influenced significantly by private decisions related to business initiative, or changing consumer income levels or tastes.
- A third reason is the great difficulty of establishing the causal factors responsible for past and current trends in non-merchandise transactions and generalizing from them to arrive at an evaluation of prospective developments.

Canada's recent currency crisis, culminating in a return to a fixed exchange rate at 92½¢ U.S. and the imposition of the so-called austerity program, has focused world-wide attention on the character and persistence of Canada's balance-of-payments deficit. The purpose of this study is to describe the broad trends in non-merchandise transactions, to uncover and assess the main forces operating to produce these trends, and to discuss in some detail the major components that comprise the broad category of non-merchandise transactions. The study will deal mainly with trends during the past decade and with transactions between Canada and the United States.

Interpretive analysis of significant trends in non-merchandise transactions requires individual consideration of the many diverse groups of activities included in the over-all total. The principal components are: travel, interest and dividends, business services, freight and shipping, inheritances and migrant funds, and miscellaneous transactions. These are dealt with in detail in Part II of this study.

The statistical data in this study have been drawn almost entirely from Canadian sources, and all dollar figures are in Canadian dollars.

General Observations Regarding Canada's Non-merchandise Transactions

One of the features of Canada's over-all non-merchandise balance of payments has been the unbroken series of deficits in the postwar period, except for a small surplus of $19 million in 1948. This consistent deficit pattern has been due principally to transactions with the United States, supplemented since 1953 by a switch from a surplus to a deficit position in transactions with overseas countries.

Due to the emergence and growth of the deficit with overseas countries, the non-merchandise deficit with the United States declined as a percentage

2

of the total, from over 80 percent in 1953 to about 65 percent in 1960-62. In a contrary trend, the deficit with the United Kingdom increased from 7 percent of the total in 1955 to about 13 percent in 1960-62, while that with other overseas countries rose from 2 percent of the total in 1953 to well over 20 percent in 1960-62. In terms of rates of growth per annum since 1953 the record is shown in Table 1.

TABLE 1

Annual Rate of Growth of Canada's Non-merchandise Receipts, Payments and Deficits

(Compound annual rates in percentage)

	1953-62			1957-62		
	Receipts	Payments	Deficit	Receipts	Payments	Deficit
All countries..................	4.5	6.3	11.0	4.1	3.7	3.1
United States.................	4.2	5.4	8.0	4.8	3.3	0.2
United Kingdom..............	3.0	5.0	9.5	2.1	3.8	7.2
All other countries............	6.5	12.0	43.0	2.6	5.7	11.2

In the period 1953-62 non-merchandise receipts increased by 4.5 percent per annum compared to 6.3 percent per annum for payments. Since 1957, however, the growth in receipts has declined slightly to 4.1 percent per annum while the growth in payments has fallen to 3.7 percent per annum.

In dollar terms, interest, dividend, and business service payments have been the major contributor to the over-all deficit, particularly with the United States. These payments have been relatively unimportant to overseas countries. The large percentage increase in the deficit with overseas countries has been due mainly to an increase in travel, government, institutional, and personal payments.

For the three years 1958-60, deficits on travel account displaced business services as the second most important contributor to deficits. A sharp decline in the travel deficit occurred in 1961 and again in 1962, when a surplus of $90 million with the United States was achieved.

TABLE 2

Percentage Changes in Selected Canadian Economic Indicators, 1949-61

(Calculated from peaks and troughs of the business cycle, on a seasonally adjusted basis)

	1949-53 Trough to Peak	1953-54 Peak to Trough	1954-57 Trough to Peak	1957-58 Peak to Trough	1958-60 Trough to Peak	1960-61 Peak to Trough
Gross national product..............	+ 50.5	− 2.4	+ 29.4	+ 3.3	+ 9.5	− 1.2
Consumer expenditures.............	+ 39.1	+ 2.8	+ 22.4	+ 7.1	+ 8.5	+ 4.1
Index of industrial production.......	+ 26.7	− 0.8	+ 25.2	− 2.5	+ 10.3	− 2.9
Exports of goods...................	+ 40.3	− 9.7	+ 25.1	+ 2.1	+ 12.7	− 1.2
Imports of goods..................	+ 63.7	− 7.6	+ 43.9	− 15.1	+ 15.4	− 4.8
Non-merchandise receipts...........	+ 28.5	− 5.0	+ 30.0	− 8.9	+ 12.5	+ 0.2
Non-merchandise payments..........	+ 55.8	− 2.2	+ 42.9	− 0.4	+ 12.4	+ 9.9
Interest and dividend receipts........	+122.2	− 11.1	− 9.0	+ 27.3	+ 11.9	− 2.2
Interest and dividend payments......	+ 35.1	− 11.1	+ 35.6	+ 4.3	+ 12.9	+ 34.3
Travel receipts....................	+ 11.8	− 1.3	+ 21.3	− 3.4	+ 15.9	+ 7.8
Travel payments...................	+ 84.0	+ 4.3	+ 37.5	−	+ 16.7	+ 5.2
All other receipts..................	+ 25.0	− 5.3	+ 40.5	− 16.6	+ 11.4	− 2.4
All other payments................	+ 56.6	− 8.2	+ 49.3	− 2.7	+ 10.3	−

While both non-merchandise payments and receipts have fluctuated in sympathy with the business cycle, payments have shown increasing insensitivity to the business cycle, especially during downswings in the cycle. This was particularly evident in the business decline of 1960-61 when payments increased by 9.9 percent compared to a decline of 2.9 percent in industrial production and 4.8 percent in commodity imports. The amplitude of the fluctuations in non-merchandise payments and receipts has almost always been smaller than that for merchandise trade.

Payments for interest, dividends, and travel (which comprise roughly 40 percent of the total) have shown marked insensitivity to declining phases of the business cycle. In this respect, changes in travel expenditures have corresponded more closely to changes in consumer expenditures than to the general level of business activity. As might have been expected, other components of non-merchandise payments, such as freight and shipping, business services and miscellaneous income, have fluctuated more closely with business activity. The insensitivity of interest payments is explained by two factors: the contractual nature of such payments; and the fact that the periods of heaviest Canadian borrowing in New York (and, to a lesser extent, foreign investment in Canada) occur late in the business upswing when relatively tighter credit conditions and higher interest rates prevail. As a result interest payments tend to increase during the subsequent business decline.

One might suppose that dividend payments would be quite responsive to fluctuations in business activity. In fact, however, they have proved to be only slightly less insensitive than interest payments. Several factors account for this pattern. In the first place, the steady growth in foreign investment in Canada of an equity nature has tended to obscure any significant cyclical fluctuations in dividend payments. Perhaps more important is the fact that the trend of earnings has been only one, and at times a secondary, consideration in the determination of dividend policy and payments. Over the past five years, dividends paid by internationally controlled companies in Canada have averaged just over 50 percent of earnings. During most of the postwar period, dividend policy has been closely geared to the need of the subsidiary for working or investment capital. In a period of declining business activity or investment opportunity there is a tendency for some companies to remit idle funds to the parent company by means of increased dividend payments. At other times, changes in taxes or concern about the future exchange value of the Canadian dollar have been dominant considerations in the determination of dividend policy.

While travel expenditures have proved to be responsive to the stimulation of business expansions, they have exhibited some resistance to contraction in business activity. In this respect they appear to reflect the trend in consumer spending. Other components of non-merchandise transactions excluding government transactions, official contributions, and gold exports appear to fluctuate in line with the business cycle.

Without overstressing the relationship, it is clear that on balance non-merchandise transactions respond rather sluggishly to fluctuations in business, particularly during contractions, and this characteristic could complicate the problem of following appropriate anticyclical monetary and fiscal policies under conditions of a fixed exchange rate.

PART I
The Broad Pattern of
Non-merchandise Transactions

2

Early Patterns of
Non-merchandise Transactions

TABLE 3
Canada's Balance of Non-merchandise Transactions
(Millions of Dollars)

	1926		1930		1936		1946	
	All Countries	U.S.	All Countries	U.S.	All Countries	U.S.	All Countries	U.S.
Net exports of gold............	30	30	39	39	132	132	96	96
Tourist and travel..............	53	70	88	100	67	75	86	86
Interest and dividends..........	−208	−126	−287	−195	−236	−191	−242	−203
Freight and shipping...........	− 9	− 21	− 33	− 28	− 17	− 12	92	− 68
All other.....................	− 38	− 8	− 49	− 23	− 44	− 22	−143	− 88
Total.....................	*−172*	*− 55*	*−242*	*−107*	*− 98*	*− 18*	*−111*	*−177*

A review of the prewar pattern of non-merchandise trade reveals consistent surpluses from tourist travel and the export of gold, and deficits for all other items in the balance. The appearance of a surplus on freight and shipping in 1946 reflects the build-up of shipping facilities during the war. During the period, the increasing importance of U.S. capital in developing Canada and repatriation of debt held in the United Kingdom are reflected in the fact that interest and dividend payments to the United States increased by 80 percent compared to an increase of only 30 percent to all countries. Increasing exports of nonmonetary gold became a significant factor in the balance of payments in the mid-1930s and reached a peak in 1941 of $204 million. During the war, gold production and exports were severely curtailed and prewar levels were not approached until 1950 when exports

9

totaled $163 million. Since that time the pressure of increasing costs against a fixed selling price has discouraged production and despite the payment of subsidies, gold exports have stabilized at around the 1950 level.

The relationship between non-merchandise and merchandise receipts and payments is given in the following table:

TABLE 4

Canada's Non-merchandise Receipts and Payments as a Percentage of Merchandise Receipts and Payments

	1926		1930		1936		1946	
	All Countries	U.S.	All Countries	U.S.	All Countries	U.S.	All Countries	U.S.
Non-merchandise receipts as a % of exports	28	65	43	85	36	100	40	65
Non-merchandise payments as a % of imports	58	56	68	70	93	110	60	57

It is interesting to note that in 1946 the ratio of non-merchandise receipts and payments to exports and imports, with respect to the United States, were virtually identical to those of 1926. In the intervening years, however, at least up to the war, non-merchandise transactions, particularly with the United States, increased considerably faster than merchandise trade. The rapid expansion of both exports and imports during the war was the principal factor in restoring the 1946 ratios to the 1926 level.

For all countries during this early period, the non-merchandise account was more important on the payments than the receipts side of the balance of payments, whereas the reverse was generally true for U.S. transactions. This was due in part to the large favourable balance on travel account with the United States and large exports of gold.

The prewar pattern of non-merchandise transactions can be summarized as follows:

(1) Important surpluses on travel account, particularly with the United States.

(2) A large increase in gold exports in the mid-1930s that came close to wiping out the non-merchandise deficit.

(3) The shift in interest and dividend payments to the United States was a more important trend than the moderate rise in total payments.

(4) Freight and shipping produced small deficits which were reversed in the early postwar years from the operations of the war-expanded merchant marine.

(5) The miscellaneous category, comprising payments for business services, institutional and personal remittances (including migrant funds) and entertainment, particularly film rental, increased steadily throughout the period.

10

3

Postwar Changes in
Non-merchandise Transactions

The postwar relationship between merchandise and non-merchandise transactions is shown in the top chart on the inside front cover of this study, and in detail in Appendix Table 36. Rates of growth over the period have been as follows:

TABLE 5

Annual Rates of Growth in Canadian Merchandise
and Non-merchandise Transactions
(Percent)

	1946-62	1951-62
Exports	6.25	4.50
Non-merchandise receipts	4.50	4.50
Imports	8.00	3.87
Non-merchandise payments	6.00	6.00

These figures show that in contrast with a relatively high and steady growth in non-merchandise receipts and payments over the entire postwar period, there has been a marked decline in the rate of growth of merchandise trade. Since 1951, non-merchandise payments have grown much faster than imports. The relationship between merchandise and non-merchandise transactions for the years 1956 to 1962, a period of slower growth for Canada, is shown in Table 6. The dramatic improvement in 1962 is clearly evident.

TABLE 6

Index Numbers of Canadian Merchandise and Non-merchandise Transactions, 1957-62
(1956=100)

Year	Exports	Non-merchandise Receipts	Imports	Non-merchandise Payments
1957	101.2	99.6	98.6	109.6
1958	101.0	95.3	91.0	110.5
1959	106.5	100.9	100.2	120.3
1960	111.5	105.6	99.6	124.2
1961	121.7	113.4	102.7	132.6
1962	131.6	121.9	111.6	131.9

Canada earned its only postwar surplus ($19 million) on non-merchandise transactions with all countries in 1948. From 1948 through 1961, with a minor reversal in 1952, deficits increased yearly to reach a peak of $1,155 million in 1961. A 13 percent decline to a figure of $1,003 million occurred in 1962. The major trends contributing to this pattern have been: a swing from a surplus to a deficit for travel expenditures, freight and shipping, and migrant funds; and increased deficits for interest and dividend payments, business services, and miscellaneous transactions. The postwar trends in non-merchandise transactions with all countries, and with the United States, are shown in the bottom chart inside the front cover of this study. More detailed charts on the main components of such transactions are shown on the inside back cover.

Approximately one half of the increase in the over-all deficit since 1948 is accounted for by transactions with the United States. Transactions with the United Kingdom accounted for roughly one third. Interest and dividend payments, business services, and freight and shipping were the most important contributors to the deficit with the United States.

TABLE 7

Accumulated Canadian Non-merchandise Deficits With All Countries, 1946-62
(Millions of Dollars)

Travel expenditures	$1,024
Interest and dividends	6,262
Freight and shipping	427
Inheritances and migrant funds	279
Gold production	−2,464[a]
All other	4,058[b]
Total Accumulated Deficit	$9,586

[a] Surplus.
[b] Includes $2,216 million accumulated deficit for business services from 1950.

TABLE 8

Accumulated Canadian Non-merchandise Deficits With the United States, 1946-62
(Millions of Dollars)

Travel expenditures	$ 31
Interest and dividends	5,791
Freight and shipping	1,715
Inheritances and migrant funds	744
Gold production	−2,464[a]
All other	1,664[b]
Total Accumulated Deficit	$7,481

a Surplus.
b Includes accumulated deficit of $1,876 million since 1952 for business services.
NOTE: 1962 figures for interest and dividends, freight and shipping, inheritances and migrant funds estimated.

TABLE 9

Canadian Non-merchandise Transactions With All Countries, Selected Postwar Years
(Millions of Dollars)

	1946	1951	1956	1961	1962
Travel expenditures	+ 86	− 6	−161	− 160	− 50
Interest and dividends	−242	−335	−381	− 561	− 570
Freight and shipping	+ 92	− 3	− 45	− 82	− 90
Inheritances and migrant funds	+ 30	+ 7	− 16	− 71	− 39
Business services	− 42	−165	−169	− 214	− 246
Gold production	+ 96	+150	+150	+ 162	+ 165
All other	−228	− 18	− 16	− 229	− 173
Total	−208	−370	−638	−1,155	− 1,003

TABLE 10

Canadian Non-merchandise Transactions With the United States, Selected Postwar Years
(Millions of Dollars)

	1946	1951	1956	1961	1962
Travel expenditures	+ 86	+ 12	− 82	− 24	+ 90
Interest and dividends	−203	−325	−347	−533	−529[e]
Freight and shipping	− 68	−112	−128	−103	−100[e]
Inheritances and migrant funds	− 12	− 23	− 49	− 83	− 89[e]
Business services	− 42	−165	−168	−204	−228[e]
Gold production	+ 96	+150	+150	+162	+165
All other	− 34	+ 28	+152	+ 14	+ 20[e]
Total	−177	−435	−472	−771	−641

e Estimated.

13

Among the underlying causes of Canada's growing deficit on non-merchandise transactions in the postwar period are the following:

(1) The rapid growth of the Canadian economy and the large extent to which this growth has been based on the import of investment capital and technical and administrative services.

(2) The servicing of the large inflows of capital through payment of interest and dividends, accounts in the postwar period for almost two thirds of the accumulated deficit in non-merchandise transactions with all countries and for over three quarters of the deficit with the United States.

(3) The main economic reasons for heavy foreign—principally U.S.—investment in Canada are: to develop a relatively cheap, abundant, and geographically handy source of raw and semiprocessed materials; to achieve a natural extension of the U.S. market; to hurdle Canadian tariff protection; and to operate within the British preferential tariff system. These aims, together with ease of communications and geographic proximity, influenced the retention of foreign ownership or control as an integral part of the investment decision. Control has had a decisive effect on the expansion of business service payments to U.S. parent companies. Familiarity and experience with American resources of engineering, architectural, marketing, advertising, insurance and other specialized facilities have more often than not been the deciding factor in the employment of such services. To some extent this situation has inhibited the development and expansion of Canadian facilities so that there has been some element of perpetuation of existing practice. As a result, expansion of Canadian industrial activity will continue to find reflection in an expansion of business service payments, though perhaps at a gradually slower pace.

(4) Rising levels of discretionary income in Canada have permitted larger consumer expenditures for travel, recreation, and specialized consumer services. The increasing ease and economy of foreign travel, stimulated by longer paid vacation periods, cheaper air fares, and more widespread ownership of cars have been important factors in the increase of deficits on travel account. The wide choice of consumer, cultural, recreational and other service facilities offered by the United States has understandably diverted a large share of Canadian expenditure for such items to that market. Rising incomes have also resulted in larger net payments abroad by immigrants.

(5) Expanding international trade and the growing complexity and diversity of contacts between Canada and other nations at all levels of activity have given rise to increased net payments for such items as freight and shipping, diplomatic and trade services, and defense expenditures, to name a few.

While the over-all impression is one of rigidity rather than flexibility in the pattern of payments, and the prospect of slow rather than rapid adjustment to a position of better balance, the experience of 1961, and even more particularly 1962, encourages the view that the problem of current account deficits is perhaps not as intractable as has sometimes been claimed. The improving trend in merchandise trade—from a peak postwar deficit of $728 million in 1956 to a surplus of $173 million in 1961 and a further surplus of $155 million in 1962—will in time improve Canada's balance on certain non-merchandise transactions such as freight and shipping (and, to a lesser extent, business services). The discount Canadian dollar, together with various financial and tax arrangements, should reinforce the improving trend in international trade over the intermediate term.

Another encouraging trend is the recent marked improvement in the balance on travel account. Here again the discount dollar, government action discouraging imports by travelers, and the more aggressive promotion of tourist travel to Canada—point toward continued improvement in the balance on travel account.

Most expressions of pessimism over Canada's ability to cope with its deficit on current account stress particularly the large and steadily growing deficit arising from interest and dividend payments. Even here, however, the magnitude of the task of financing such payments in the future has probably been exaggerated by its association with the problem of assessing the economic and political consequences flowing from the degree of nonresident control of the investments giving rise to such payments. Leaving aside the problem of control, which is beyond the scope of this study, a proper perspective on Canada's continuing ability to finance the current pattern of interest and dividend payments should include consideration not only of the sharply rising trend of payments but also the growth, slower though it has been of late, of domestic and foreign means to meet such payments. In the case of dividend payments, there is undoubtedly sufficient leeway over short periods to increase dividends sufficiently to be embarrassing from an exchange reserve point of view. This situation, together with the large volume of volatile short-term funds that enter into the composition of Canada's capital inflow, clearly dictate a higher level of foreign exchange reserves than would otherwise be required. From a longer-term point of view, increased dividend payments must be supported by increased earnings and these will increasingly be associated with increased exports or import-displacing domestic production, both of which activities improve Canada's ability to finance dividend payments to nonresidents.

With respect to interest payments, without defending what appears to be too heavy Canadian reliance on the U.S. capital market, the oft-cited danger that Canada will be forced to repay in U.S. funds at maturity any substantial volume of debt, ignores the well established pattern of refinancing such debt when it matures; the risk lies principally in the possibility that such refinancing may have to be done at a higher interest cost. The ratio of interest payments to various measures of ability to pay is lower than the prewar ratio. It is true nevertheless that in the past five years, interest payments have grown at a faster pace than the revenues necessary to support such payments. In such circumstances it is essential that Canadian borrowing from nonresidents be limited as far as practicable to purposes that in a direct way encourage and stimulate a faster pace of Canadian growth.

PART II

The Main Components of Canada's Non-merchandise Transactions

4

Canada's Balance of Payments on Travel Account

For a quarter of a century prior to 1951 Canada enjoyed an unbroken series of surpluses on travel account with the rest of the world. A consistently favourable balance with the United States more than offset an equally consistent, although much less substantial, series of deficits on travel expenditures with overseas countries. During the first five years following World War II, this traditional pattern of Canada's travel account reasserted itself.

TABLE 11

Canada's Deficit on Travel Expenditures by Principal Geographical Areas
(Millions of Dollars)

Deficit with	1951	1952	1953	1954	1955	1956	1957	1958	1959	1960	1961	1962
United States	+12	−37	−25	−37	− 60	− 82	− 78	−104	− 97	− 87	− 24	+ 90
United Kingdom	−12	−17	−19	−22	− 27	− 32	− 29	− 34	− 44	− 50	− 50	− 52
Other countries	− 6	−12	−19	−25	− 34	− 47	− 55	− 55	− 66	− 70	− 86	− 88
All countries	− 6	−66	−63	−84	−121	−161	−162	−193	−207	−207	−160	− 50

TABLE 12

Travel Deficit with Principal Geographical Areas as a Percentage of Canada's Total Deficit on Travel Expenditures
(Percent)

Deficit with	1952	1953	1954	1955	1956	1957	1958	1959	1960	1961
United States	56.1	39.6	44.0	49.6	50.9	48.1	53.9	46.9	42.0	15.0
United Kingdom	25.8	30.2	26.2	22.3	19.9	17.9	17.6	21.3	24.2	31.2
Other countries	18.1	30.2	29.8	28.1	29.2	34.0	28.5	31.8	33.8	53.8
All countries	100.0	100.0	100.0	100.0	100.0	100.0	100.0	100.0	100.0	100.0

The surplus position with the United States, however, began to deteriorate in 1949 and disappeared in 1952, to be followed by a progression of rising deficits that reached a peak of $104 million in 1958. During the subsequent three years, the deficit with the United States was substantially reduced, and in 1962 a surplus of $90 million was achieved.

Rising deficits with overseas countries have characterized the whole period under review, the 1962 deficit totaling $140 million. It was not until 1961 that the improving balance with the United States checked the growth in the over-all deficit. In that year, the over-all deficit dropped to $160 million from $207 million the previous year, and to $50 million in 1962. The principal reasons for early postwar surpluses on travel account with the United States are to be found in the more favourable position of Americans as compared with Canadians in this period with respect to new automobile production and ownership, and less restrictive currency regulations. An additional factor was the small volume of U.S. tourist traffic moving overseas, perhaps partly owing to austerity living conditions in Britain and Europe, but also to the fact that Americans were spending heavily for new housing and home furnishings and chose a cheaper Canadian vacation as an alternative to a more expensive overseas holiday. By contrast, Canadian travel to the United States was inhibited by currency restrictions and the relatively low density of automobile ownership. For example, between November 1947 and October 1950, Canadian pleasure travelers were restricted to $150 per year of foreign currency and it was not until February 1951 that all such restrictions were lifted.

By the early 1950s overseas travel became more comfortable as European living conditions improved, transportation became cheaper and faster with the introduction of new luxury liners and faster and larger aircraft, and rising U.S. personal incomes and longer vacation periods brought a European vacation within the grasp of a widening circle of Americans. This movement diverted some tourist traffic away from Canada. At the same time, the close personal ties that have always existed between Canadians and residents of Great Britain and many European countries, and that were broadened by contacts made during the war, stimulated a rush of Canadian tourists overseas —a movement which was proportionately even larger than in the case of U.S. tourists to overseas countries. Rising auto production and incomes in Canada and the lifting of currency restrictions for tourist travel stimulated an enormous increase in travel to the United States.

Duty free quotas for foreign goods purchased by Canadian travelers were first introduced in 1938 but were inoperative during the period of wartime exchange controls. Currency controls for pleasure travel were relaxed at a time when there was a shortage of consumer goods in Canada relative to pent up demands and consumer liquid resources, and when the availability and lower prices of American goods, particularly household appliances and clothing, made them attractive to Canadian buyers. The rapid manner in which Canadians took advantage of the duty free import privilege is illustrated by the following figures.

20

TABLE 13

Canadian Travel Expenditures on Duty Free Imports
(Millions of Dollars)

1948	$ 3.6
1949	28.8
1950	33.0
1951	47.0
1952	65.6

Under these influences, travel surpluses with both the United States and the United Kingdom turned to deficits in 1952, and these increased steadily until 1959. In that year, an improvement in the balance with the United States occurred and persisted through 1962.

By far the greater proportion of Canada's receipts and payments on travel are derived from the movement of people between the United States and Canada. But travel between Canada and overseas countries, especially on the part of Canadians, has become increasingly significant. This is illustrated by an examination of the distribution of Canada's receipts and payments on travel account by principal geographical areas. The contribution of Americans to Canada's total travel receipts has remained at a very high level declining moderately over the postwar period from almost 98 percent of total receipts in 1946 to 91 percent in 1962. Overseas travel to Canada has developed very slowly. Travelers from the United Kingdom accounted for roughly 4 percent of total receipts in 1962, compared to 1 percent in 1946, while travelers from other overseas countries contributed 5 percent of total receipts in 1962.

On the payments side, the decreasing importance of the United States as the chief recipient of Canada's travel expenditures has been more pronounced, the U.S. share having declined from 96 percent of Canada's total travel payments in 1946 to a low of 69 percent in 1962. Tourist payments to the United Kingdom and other overseas countries increased equally between 1946 and 1954 but since then, payments to the United Kingdom have declined relative to those to other overseas countries. In 1962, payments to the United Kingdom accounted for 12 percent of total payments, and all other countries roughly 19 percent.

Despite the fact that travel between Canada and the United Stares continues to account for the greater part of Canada's total receipts and payments, a proportionally much larger share of the deficit on travel account has been incurred with overseas countries. In 1962, in fact, the deficit with overseas countries totaled $140 million, compared with a surplus of $90 million with the U.S.

The increasing deficit position with overseas countries has been due largely to the growth of personal incomes in Canada during and since the Second World War. This development has vastly enlarged that group with sufficient discretionary income to spend on travel. On the nonrecreational side, moreover, the growth of Canada's export trade and the diversification of its commercial interests, its increasing participation in international affairs arising from military, economic, and diplomatic commitments and responsibilities, and the lure of cultural and educational opportunities abroad have all combined to spur travel to overseas countries.

The failure of Canada to develop reciprocal tourist trade with overseas countries to the same extent as with the United States is attributable partly to the facts of geography—the long distances and time factor involved. Even more important has been the relatively low level of incomes in overseas countries, the relatively low external purchasing power of many foreign currencies in terms of the Canadian dollar, and, until recently, the severe currency restrictions applying to overseas travelers of many of these countries (especially to such dollar countries as Canada and the United States). It is interesting to note that recent trends—rising incomes in Europe, the devalued Canadian dollar, and the great relaxation in currency restrictions—have lowered to some extent the barriers to overseas tourist travel to Canada. Nevertheless, as evidenced by the experience with U.S. visitors, half of whom visit this country in the third quarter of the year, Canada up to now has had a very seasonal and limited appeal, and one which is largely directed to the outdoors traveler. For these reasons alone, it seems unlikely that, insofar as overseas visitors are concerned, Canada will easily or quickly develop into a region of mass tourist appeal as it has become for Americans. However, as cheaper and faster means of overseas transportation are developed, as vacation periods are lengthened, and as Canadian tourist facilities and attractions are broadened and upgraded, a steady increase in overseas tourist traffic can be visualized.

Travel by Americans to Canada has become highly developed over the past quarter century and continues to grow. The reasons are obvious and stem from such factors as geographical proximity, language, similarities (but also differences) in culture and tastes, the development of personal and business ties in each country, good political and economic relations, and the mass ownership of the automobile. These factors have also operated to stimulate mass Canadian travel to the United States. In Canada's case, however, climate has played a stronger initiating role in tourist travel, while over the past ten years the increasing density of car ownership in Canada has been another important factor. Passenger car registrations in Canada increased by close to 8 percent annually over the 1950-60 period, compared with slightly over 4 percent in the United States. Although by 1960 there was only one passenger car for every 4.5 persons in Canada (compared with one automobile for every 2.9 in the United States), the difference of 1.6 persons per automobile was significantly narrower than the spread of 3.5 in 1950 and of 5.0 in 1946. This growth in automobile ownership has vastly expanded the horizons of travel for Canadians visiting the United States. Since 1955, for example, between 75 and 80 percent of Canadians entering the United States have traveled by car. In 1961, the figure was 80 percent and accounted for 52 percent of Canadian tourist expenditures in the United States. Estimates of the percentage distribution of Canadian travel to the United States, by purpose of trip, for 1961 are shown in Table 14.

22

TABLE 14

Estimates of Canadian Travel to the United States by Purpose of Trip, 1961

Recreation......................	48.6%
Visiting friends and relatives........	32.1%
Business.......................	10.3%
Shopping.......................	5.9%
All other......................	3.1%

Source: *Travel Between Canada and Other Countries*, 1961, Dominion Bureau of Statistics, Ottawa.

It is interesting to note that in relation to the size of the respective populations of the two countries, far more Canadians visit the United States than the reverse. Furthermore, partly reflecting the factors discussed above, the increase in the number of Canadians visiting the United States since the war has been much greater than the increase in the number of Americans visiting Canada. This arises from the fact that with the greater part of Canada's population residing within easy reach of the border, Canadians are more responsive to the influence of the many media of communications between the United States and Canada and to the recreational and shopping advantages to be found across the border. It is unlikely that such considerations have a comparable impact upon the travel inclinations of the mass of U.S. residents except, perhaps, in some border areas. In 1961, border crossings by Americans entering Canada totaled 30.5 million, an increase of only 7 million from the 1950 figure. By comparison, however, the 29.3 million border crossings of Canadians into the United States represented an increase of 13.3 million over the 1950 total.

Not only has the annual influx of U.S. visitors increased very moderately, but the per capita expenditure of this group has also shown almost no signs of growth over the past decade, ranging normally between $10 and $12, although it jumped sharply to $14.3 in 1961. On the other hand, the substantial growth in Canadian visits to the United States was accompanied by a steady increase in expenditures per visitor, from $12 per visit in 1950 to a high of $16 in 1959. In 1960 and 1961, reflecting the declining value of the Canadian dollar and the smaller price advantage to Canadians of shopping in the United States, expenditures per person declined to $15.5. The recent lowering of the dollar amount of tourist purchases allowed free entry into Canada from the United States—from $100 to $25 every three months—will almost certainly induce a further decline.

Much of this differential in expenditures per visitor must be attributed to the fact that the destinations of those Canadians visiting the United States for more than 48 hours tend to take them further into that country, and to keep them there longer, than do the destinations of the same category of Americans visiting Canada. For example, in 1960, travel to the State of Florida increased sufficiently to raise it from a position of third most popular destination in 1959 among longer-term visitors to the second most popular

23

destination, after the State of New York. It is estimated that 13 percent of all Canadians in the longer-term group visiting the United States in that year traveled to Florida. Visitors passing less than 48 hours in either country, a category which consistently has accounted for well over 80 percent of total visitors, have generally had expenditures averaging between $2 and $3.6 per visit. Expenditures per visitor remaining longer than 48 hours, however, have been significantly larger. Over the 1950-59 period, expenditures per visit of Americans remaining in Canada over 48 hours ranged between $50 and $58 whereas the per capita expenditures of Canadian visitors in the same category ranged between $75 and $90.

Another contribution to Canada's travel deficit with the United States has been the high degree of concentration of U.S. visits to this country in the third quarter of the year—almost half the total annual visits from the United States occur during this quarter. This tends to place a limit on the numbers which can be absorbed and carries with it the immense problem of providing profitably a high standard of accommodation and amenities for a huge number of visitors over a short period, particularly when most of the overnight groups remain for only one or two nights.

Apart from these considerations, tourist travel to Canada, particularly from the United States, has been discouraged by the development of competitive attractions both in the United States and abroad. In addition, increasing personal and family contacts, connected with the heavy inflow of immigrants from Europe since the war, and the development of similar contacts through military service during and since the war, have had their impact upon the growth of Canadian and American travel overseas. Although the numbers of travelers involved are minute compared with those traveling across the Canadian-U.S. border, such overseas visits are more expensive and, generally, of much longer duration. In 1960, Canadian visitors to the United Kingdom, who accounted for 30 percent of total overseas trips, spent an average of 50 days on their trip. Furthermore, use of foreign transportation facilities contributes heavily to the deficit with foreign countries, and in 1960, for example, accounted for 32 percent of all overseas expenditures by Canadians returning directly to Canada. Thus, in that year Canadian transportation facilities received only 44 percent of the total transportation payments to both foreign and domestic carriers. The increasing popularity of air travel, in which Canadian carriers are in a better position to participate than in travel by ship, may be a factor tempering the expansion of the deficit on travel account.

The travel deficit appears to have peaked out in 1959 and 1960 as indicated by the significant declines in 1961 and 1962. Moreover, the outlook for a continuing reduction in Canada's travel deficit is promising. Over the past five years there has been a marked deceleration in the rate of growth of Canada's total travel payments compared with the growth rate experienced over the past decade—from 6.0 percent compounded annually over the 1952-62 period to approximately 3 percent per annum during the 1957-62 period. On the other hand, there has been a modest acceleration in the rate of growth of Canadian travel receipts from just over 7 percent compounded annually over the decade, compared with 9 percent per annum during the past five years. Recent austerity measures and the discount on the Canadian dollar have both stimulated American travel in Canada and sharply reduced Canadian tourist purchases in the United States. Furthermore, the continued improvement in the standard of living in European countries, combined with the implementation of plans to encourage European vacation travel to North America, should both prove beneficial to Canada.

While it is not intended that this study make policy recommendations regarding means to reduce deficits in non-merchandise transactions, an analysis of recent trends in tourist travel does reveal some rather interesting subjects for further study.

As far as U.S. visitors are concerned, the principal difficulties standing in the way of increased travel and expenditures are the following:

(1) The relatively short, warm weather travel period that concentrates the bulk of U.S. tourist travel into the third quarter of the year. This places a heavy physical and economic strain on tourist facilities, with the annual income of such facilities being very largely compressed into a period of four or five months.

(2) The emphasis on Canada as an outdoor vacation land which aggravates the summer congestion and appeals heavily to campers who are typically light spenders.

(3) The scarcity of first rate tourist attractions and accommodations that would lure American tourists further from the border and stimulate larger expenditures.

(4) For the overseas visitor, the scarcity of medium priced accommodations and particularly the very few well-run packaged bus tours of the quality existing in Britain and on the Continent. Rising incomes in Europe and the prospects of cheaper and faster transportation suggest that the potential for increased European tourist travel in Canada is significant.

To even out the concentration of tourist travel in the school vacation months, attention should be switched to attracting adults. There are at least two interesting avenues of approach to this problem:

(a) More emphasis on conventions. Convention business is ideal for Canada. It gets away from the summer congestion. It means a length of stay well above the current average, and it usually involves people on expense accounts and with larger personal funds to spend. Present facilities are taxed to the limit and expansion of this type of accommodation deserves a high priority.

(b) More cultural appeals for American tourists. The Stratford Festival has shown the possibilities in this approach. The ingredients are already present in Canada's major cities to organize and operate Festivals in the fields of music, theatre, and art at different periods throughout the year. High quality is the essence of success in this approach. Such a development would cut the travel deficit in two ways—by encouraging tourist travel to Canada and by keeping Canadian tourists at home.

The planning now under way to celebrate the centenary of Canadian Confederation in 1967, and to hold the World's Fair in Montreal in the same year, provides an unparalleled opportunity to lay the foundations for a broader, more imaginative, and better diversified program of tourist attractions and accommodations.

5

Interest and Dividends

The largest single influence in the expansion of Canada's deficit on non-merchandise transactions since the war has been the sharp increase in non-resident investments in Canada, these having grown much faster than Canada's external assets. In fact, the consequent net payments of interest and dividends on this investment have usually been the largest single contributor to Canada's over-all current account deficit, the only exceptions in the past decade being in 1956 and 1957 when merchandise deficits were larger. Although the deficit on interest and dividend account has more than doubled from $242 million in 1946 to $570 million in 1962, it has been declining as a percentage of the total non-merchandise deficit, accounting for slightly less than half in 1961 compared to over 100 percent prior to 1951. However, in 1962, the percentage increased to 57 percent.

Interest and dividend payments are currently a much smaller percentage both of the Gross National Product and total current account receipts than was typical for the years prior to World War II. Since the end of the War the ratios have been remarkably steady with only a slight tendency for interest and dividend payments to grow faster than G.N.P. and current receipts as shown in Table 15.

TABLE 15

Ratio of Canadian Interest and Dividend Payments to Nonresidents to Gross National Product and Receipts on Current Account, Selected Years[1]

	1 Interest and Dividend Payments	2 G.N.P.	3 Current Receipts	Ratio 1:2	Ratio 1:3
	(millions of dollars)			(percent)	
1926-29........	272	5,720	1,683	4.7	16.2
1930-38........	300	4,583	1,161	6.5	25.9
1939-45........	279	9,401	3,189	3.0	8.8
1946-50........	368	14,897	3,929	2.5	9.4
1951-55........	435	24,425	5,700	1.8	7.6
1956..........	523	30,098	6,621	1.7	7.9
1957..........	587	31,443	6,625	1.9	8.9
1958..........	612	32,894	6,579	1.9	9.3
1959..........	671	34,915	6,792	1.9	9.9
1960..........	653	36,254	7,110	1.8	9.2
1961..........	770	37,421	7,734	2.1	10.0
1962..........	781	40,401	8,348	1.9	9.4

[1] 1957 and prior taken from Hugh G. L. Aitken, *American Capital and Canadian Resources*, Harvard University Press, 1961, 63.

During the postwar period, Canada's net payments position with the United States has accounted for a very large part of the total deficit on interest and dividends. While the United States has normally provided between 47 and 62 percent of Canada's receipts, it has been the most important beneficiary of Canada's interest and dividend payments, having received over 80 percent of the total in every year. Consequently, the deficit with the United States has been large, equivalent to over 84 percent of the total deficit on this item in every year, and to over 90 percent in the majority of years.

Deficits on interest and dividend transactions with overseas countries have occurred in every year since World War II, owing to a deficit position with the United Kingdom which, while small compared with Canada's deficit with the United States, has been sufficiently large to offset the small surpluses earned with other overseas countries. While the $24 million surplus earned from these other overseas countries in 1961 was fairly typical of those earned in much of the period under discussion, the disappearance of the surplus in 1958 and 1960 suggests that Canada's favourable balance with these countries is not as firmly entrenched as it appeared to be in earlier years.

The figures in Table 16 show the breakdown of the interest and dividend deficits since 1950. It will be observed that while the deficits arising from dividend payments have been considerably larger than those arising from interest payments, the latter have been growing faster in recent years and were equivalent to 36 percent of the total interest and dividend deficit in 1962.

TABLE 16
Canada's Deficits on Interest and Dividends
(Millions of Dollars)

	1950	1951	1952	1953	1954	1955	1956	1957	1958	1959	1960	1961	1962
Dividends	303	275	213	181	199	250	291	325	326	349	319	381	365
Interest	81	60	55	58	77	73	90	110	118	140	161	180	205
Total	384	335	268	239	276	323	381	435	444	489	480	561	570

Interest

Canada's deficit on interest payments arises almost exclusively from transactions with the United States. Furthermore, as Table 17 shows, the occasional deficits with overseas countries have generally been as insignificant as the more frequent surpluses. The deficits incurred with the United Kingdom in 1956 and 1957 are entirely attributable to Britain's suspension of interest payment on a postwar loan, during a period of exchange crisis. The declining trend in over-all deficits prior to 1953 can be attributed to a fall in the level of payments from 1946 until 1949 accompanied by rising receipts which almost doubled in 1951 when servicing of postwar loans began.

Declining interest payments from 1946 to 1949 reflected in part the repatriation of Canadian debt owned by nonresidents during and after the war, and in part the lower interest rates prevailing at the end of the war and the change in the official selling rate of the U.S. dollar from $1.10½ to $1.00½ in July 1946. Under such circumstances, many debtors were persuaded to refund debt, including obligations payable in foreign currencies. In 1946 and 1947, for example, net retirements after new issues of foreign-held securities amounted to $590 million, including $460 million to the United States.

Although the deficit arising from interest payments continued to decline between 1949 and 1952, the reason was different from the earlier period. Interest payments actually rose as U.S. investment in Canada increased, especially through Canadian borrowing in New York spurred by tight credit conditions in Canada, but they were more than offset by receipts of interest on newly granted Canadian government loans to overseas countries.

In 1945 and 1946, $2 billion of postwar credits were provided by Canada to finance Canadian exports of goods and services to other countries or to make it possible for overseas countries to meet transitional postwar deficits in their balance of payments, to maintain adequate reserves, and to assume the obligations of multilateral trade. In the period between 1946 and 1950, credits of $1.6 billion were extended, including almost $1.2 billion to the United Kingdom under a loan negotiated in March 1946.

Servicing of the loan to the United Kingdom did not commence until 1950, with the result that interest receipts from the United Kingdom in 1951 jumped to $24 million from around $1 million in previous years. In total, receipts from all countries increased from $28 million to $54 million in that year.

During the postwar period, receipts from other overseas countries, largely servicing of postwar government loans, have remained almost static at between $13 million and $16 million a year, the lower figure having been

29

TABLE 17

Canada's Deficits on Interest Payments
(Millions of Dollars)

	1946	1950	1951	1952	1953	1954	1955	1956	1957	1958	1959	1960	1961
With the United States	− 93	− 79	− 80	− 73	− 77	− 93	− 92	− 86	−102	−129	−148	−164	−185
With the United Kingdom	− 20	− 14	+ 9	+ 8	+ 8	+ 7	+ 9	− 14	− 15	+ 7	+ 4	+ 6	+ 8
With all other countries	+ 1	+ 12	+ 11	+ 10	+ 11	+ 9	+ 10	+ 10	+ 7	+ 4	+ 4	− 3	− 3
Total deficit	−112	− 81	− 60	− 55	− 58	− 77	− 73	− 90	−110	−118	−140	−161	−180

TABLE 18

Transactions in Canadian Bonds and Debentures Between Canada and Other Countries
(Millions of Dollars)

	1952	1953	1954	1955	1956	1957	1958	1959	1960	1961	1962
Proceeds of new bond issues (payable optionally or solely in foreign currency)	260	241	244	45	508	638	494	523	298	363	571
Proceeds of new bond issues payable in Canadian dollars	33	48	68	58	89	99	140	137	123	123	122
Total proceeds of new issues	293	289	312	103	597	737	634	660	421	486	693
Trade in outstanding issues	−165	− 52	− 66	−165	+ 11	− 45	—	+ 91	+ 3	+ 63	+ 64
Gross receipts from nonresidents	128	237	246	− 62	608	692	634	751	424	549	757
Retirements	− 88	−135	−194	−178	−135	−108	−140	−241	−256	−244	−262
Net receipts from nonresidents	40	102	52	−240	473	584	494	510	168	305	495

NOTE: Minus signs signify outflow of capital from Canada.

Sources: *The Canadian Balance of International Payments*, annual issues 1952 to 1960, and *Quarterly Estimates of the Canadian Balance of International Payments*, March 1963, Dominion Bureau of Statistics, Ottawa.

realized in 1960. Canada's interest payments to these countries, however, which until 1957 had been running at between $4 million and $5 million a year, began to climb and reached a postwar high of $17 million in 1961. This trend reflected a growing volume of funds (mainly European) repatriated from colonial areas and reinvested in Canada.

The deficit position with the United States showed no real signs of growth until 1956. Interest receipts from the United States rose from $8 million in 1946 to $11 million in 1950, then moved to a slightly higher plateau, fluctuating between $15 million and $27 million a year until 1958. The rate of increase picked up again in 1959 and receipts totaled $40 million in 1961. Payments, on the other hand, after growing slowly from $90 million in 1950 to $107 million in 1956, increased at a faster pace to a level of $225 million in 1961.

The reversal in 1950 of the trend toward lower interest payments arose from a number of factors relating to capital movements at that time. Large-scale borrowings were resumed in the U.S. market, stimulated by profitable investment opportunities in Canada. The terms of borrowing were relatively more favourable in the United States, particularly in 1951, following the introduction of credit restraint in Canada. Rising interest rates on new issues in the United States in 1951 and 1952, and a lower value for the Canadian dollar in 1950 and 1951 compared with the earlier postwar years, were also factors in the rising level of interest payments.

In recent years, growing interest payments on Canadian bonds and debentures owned by nonresidents has been, to a major extent, the result of additions to nonresident holdings of Canadian bonds and debentures—largely through participation in new bond issues from 1956 through 1959, particularly in foreign currency offerings. Table 18 illustrates the large annual increment to these nonresident owned holdings.

In most years the United States has been the major participant in these transactions, normally accounting for over 85 percent of the net increase in nonresident holdings of Canadian bonds.

The unusually heavy borrowings from nonresidents in the 1956-59 period reflected domestic demands for capital in excess of the current rate of saving. A restrictive monetary policy, shaped by fears of developing inflationary pressures, further raised the cost and reduced the availability of capital funds in Canada. The U.S. bond market, on the other hand, offered not only lower interest costs but, even more important, a ready source of funds for Canadian borrowers. Reflecting large-scale investment in manufacturing and resource industries, corporations were the largest single source of demand upon external capital resources until 1958, although the provinces and municipalities also made heavy demands (see Table 19).

The sharp reduction of Canadian borrowing in external markets in 1960 and 1961 was a reflection of several factors operating with varying effect during this period:
- The cyclical decline in business activity ending in the first quarter of 1961.

- The absence of large resource projects which were such a stimulus to foreign debt creation in the previous three years.
- Government discouragement of Canadian borrowing in New York.
- The increase in the withholding tax on interest income to most non-residents in December 1960.
- Greater availability of Canadian funds as a result of an easier money policy.
- The declining trend in the U.S. value of the Canadian dollar and some uncertainty on the part of foreign investors as to the future direction of Canadian monetary and exchange policy.
- A significant narrowing of the spread in yield between the Canadian and U.S. bond markets in the latter part of 1961.

Two principal factors appear to determine the scale of U.S. bond investment in Canada or Canadian borrowing in New York. The first concerns the opportunities for profitable investment in Canadian resource, industrial or commercial development. While a large percentage of such investment is made in equity form, when the developments are large or involve utility-type operations that can support high debt ratios, a large proportion of the financing is in bond form.

The second important factor influencing the volume of foreign borrowing is the relative cost and availability of money in domestic versus foreign markets. The accompanying charts show the yield spread between Canadian and U.S. industrial bonds since 1955 and the pattern of industrial bond yields in Canada over the same period. The volume of Canadian borrowing in New York is also indicated. It will be noted that periods of high interest rates in Canada coincide roughly with periods of wide yield spread between the Canadian and U.S. bond market and with periods of expanded borrowing by Canadians in New York.

Even more important than relative yield cost has been the ready availability of funds in the United States for the purchase of Canadian bonds, mainly in issues payable in U.S. dollars, but increasingly in issues payable in Canadian dollars only. To tap available U.S. funds, at times of credit tightness in Canada particularly, Canadian borrowers have been willing to sell U.S. pay bonds at yields within 0.5 percent of a comparable issue payable in Canadian funds.

Over the intermediate term, the outlook favours an increased inflow of foreign bond investment. The financing of such projects as the Montreal subway, the development of the Columbia and Peace Rivers, and the nationalization of electric power in Quebec, will require large amounts of foreign bond money. In addition, a prospective active program of public construction at the municipal and provincial level will find Canadian borrowers in the New York market for a portion of their money requirements. At least for the near term, the discount dollar, the necessity to build up exchange reserves, and the federal government's blessing for such borrowing, has removed earlier restraint against this particular type of borrowing.

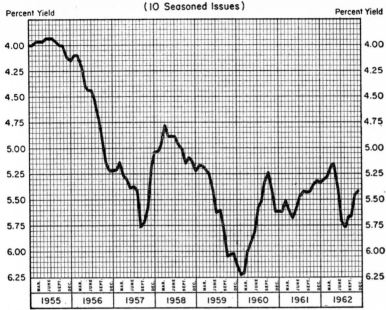

INVERTED YIELD – CANADIAN INDUSTRIAL BONDS
(10 Seasoned Issues)

Source: McLeod, Young Weir & Co., Ltd.—10 Industrial Bonds.

YIELD SPREAD BETWEEN CANADIAN
AND U.S. INDUSTRIAL BONDS (unadjusted for exchange)
AND GROSS NEW CANADIAN FOREIGN CURRENCY ISSUES
(Seasoned Issues)

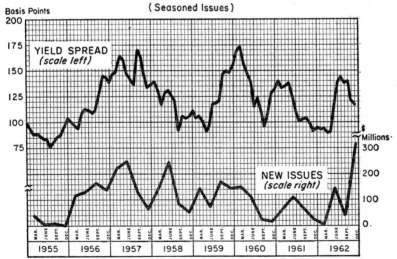

Note: 100 basis points equal 1 percent.
Sources: Yield spread—Moody's Aa Industrial Bond Index; and McLeod, Young Weir—10 Industrial Bonds.
New issues—Statistical Summary, Bank of Canada.

33

TABLE 19

Gross New Issues of Bonds and Debentures of Canadian Borrowers in Canadian Dollars and Other Currencies

(Gross new issues delivered in millions of dollars)

Year	Government of Canada, Direct and Guaranteed Bonds[1]			Provinces Direct and Guaranteed Bonds			Municipalities Direct and Guaranteed Bonds			Corporate Bonds[2]			Total Gross New Issues[3]			Total Net New Issues[4]		
	$Can.	Other	Total	$Can.	Other	Total	$Can.	Other	Total	$Can.	Other	Total	$Can.	Other	Total	$Can.	Other	Total
1955	1,370	—	1,370	371	—	371	302	42	344	689	9	698	2,732	51	2,783	1,238	−132	1,106
1956	1,527	—	1,527	420	214	634	247	108	355	813	229	1,042	3,007	551	3,558	572	367	939
1957	2,602	—	2,602	633	133	766	292	123	415	800	410	1,210	4,327	666	4,993	1,206	455	1,661
1958	9,200	—	9,200	560	166	726	379	148	527	786	209	995	10,925	523	11,448	2,553	443	2,996
1959	2,893	—	2,893	571	323	894	363	146	509	426	64	490	4,253	533	4,786	872	218	1,090
1960	2,665	—	2,665	682	87	769	492	122	614	622	96	718	4,461	305	4,766	1,664	97	1,761
1961	3,429	—	3,429	1,134	30	1,164	460	29	489	600	232	832	5,623	291	5,914	2,407	44	2,451
1962	3,307	135	3,442	975	113	1,088	453	56	509	549	210	759	5,284	514	5,798	1,374	346	1,720

[1] Excludes treasury bills, treasury notes, and deposit certificates.
[2] Excludes commercial paper with original maturity of less than one year.
[3] Excludes Canadian pay issues of I.B.R.D., Australia, and religious institutions.
[4] Gross new issues delivered less retirements.

Source: Bank of Canada, *Statistical Summary Supplement*, 1961, pp. 91-93, and *Statistical Summary*, February 1963, pp. 103-5.

TABLE 20

Canada's Balance of Payments on Dividends With Other Countries

(Millions of Dollars)

Country	1946	1950	1951	1952	1953	1954	1955	1956	1957	1958	1959	1960	1961
United States	−110	−282	−245	−186	−156	−183	−218	−261	−283	−271	−300	−265	−348
United Kingdom	− 27	− 34	− 36	− 35	− 37	− 34	− 43	− 45	− 53	− 51	− 59	− 57	− 60
Other countries	+ 7	+ 13	+ 6	+ 8	+ 12	+ 18	+ 11	+ 15	+ 11	− 4	+ 10	+ 3	+ 27
All countries	−130	−303	−275	−213	−181	−199	−250	−291	−325	−326	−349	−319	−381

External borrowing in 1962 was approximately 70 percent larger than the average for the previous two years due entirely to larger borrowing of governmental authorities. Borrowing during the first half of the year was small owing to uncertainty about Canada's exchange position. But, during the latter half of the year, as extreme fears regarding the stability of the Canadian dollar evaporated with the rapid build-up in exchange reserves, American investor interest in the Canadian bond market revived in response to a number of offerings at attractive yield spreads compared to alternative U.S. investments.

The growing scarcity of attractive fixed income investments in the United States, relative to the steady accumulation of institutional funds available for investment, may well become an increasing factor in the readiness of U.S. investors to purchase Canadian bonds. The possibility that a strong movement in this direction might, however, lead to some restrictive action by the U.S. government (especially if such a movement were to coincide with a period of strains in the latter's balance-of-payments position), cannot be categorically dismissed, but appears an unlikely one.

It is not generally recognized that in only one year (1950) in the postwar period has the inflow of U.S. capital into Canada been sufficient to finance Canada's current account deficit with the United States. In 1961, the capital inflow from the United States was $182 million below net merchandise plus non-merchandise payments to the United States. The accumulated over-all deficit with the United States totaled almost $1.8 billion in the five years from 1957 through 1961.[1]

Dividends

Dividend payments arise largely from nonresident investment in direct or portfolio form in Canadian companies or subsidiaries or unincorporated branches of foreign companies. Table 20 shows the growth of Canada's deficits in dividend transactions over the postwar period.

While Canada's net interest payments declined in the early postwar years, deficits arising from dividend payments increased and by 1950 totaled $303 million.

In this period, total dividend receipts remained stable at between $50 million and $60 million a year, while total payments were on a strong upward trend from $187 million in 1946 to $366 million in 1950. In each of the next three years payments declined, falling to $283 million in 1953, while receipts experienced a rather rapid increase to $102 million in the same year. Since 1953, Canada's dividend receipts have been remarkably steady and amounted usually to just over $100 million a year. Payments, on the other hand, experienced considerable growth from 1953 to 1957, reaching $435 million in the latter year, at which level they stabilized until 1961 when they jumped to $511 million. The deficit from dividend transactions has followed a similar pattern.

---

[1] *Annual Report*, 1962, Bank of Canada, pp. 40-41.

Since 1950, net dividend payments to the United States have never account-ed for less than 83 percent of the total dividend deficit, the balance arising from transactions with the United Kingdom. In general, Canada has had a small surplus on such transactions with other overseas countries.

Since 1950, there have been no significant changes in the geographical distribution either of receipts or payments. The United States has received between 79 and 88 percent of Canada's total dividend payments, although the ratio has fluctuated narrowly around the 80 percent level in most years. Of the overseas countries, Britain has received between 10 and 17 percent of Canada's payments since 1950, and all other countries between 1.6 and 6.0 percent.

On the receipts side, there has been a somewhat wider percentage distri-bution between the United States and other overseas countries. While the United States accounted for between 57 and 76 percent of Canada's total dividend receipts between 1950 and 1961, the United Kingdom provided between 4 and 15 percent and other countries between 20 and 33 percent.

One of the striking aspects of the trend in Canada's dividend payments since 1950 is the relative lack of growth of such payments compared with the large annual increments to nonresident holdings of dividend-generating in-vestments which are shown in Table 21.

TABLE 21

Annual Increase in Book Value of Nonresident Direct and Portfolio Investment in Capital Stock of Canadian Companies and Other Corporation Assets

(Millions of Dollars)

	1950	1951	1952	1953	1954	1955	1956	1957	1958	1959	1960
Increase in investments of all nonresidents............	440	652	671	841	851	973	1,338	1,194	758	1,087	1,039
U.S. investors..............	372	548	570	694	630	683	897	867	564	880	695
U.K. investors..............	46	38	52	87	152	160	275	225	141	115 } 344
All other investors..........	22	66	49	60	69	130	166	102	53	92 }
						(Percent)					
U.S. investment as % of total..	84.5	84.3	84.9	82.6	74.0	70.2	67.0	72.6	74.4	81.0	66.9
U.K. investment as % of total..	10.5	5.5	7.8	10.3	17.9	16.4	20.6	18.8	18.6	10.6 } 33.1
Other investment as % of total.	5.0	10.2	7.3	7.1	8.1	13.4	12.4	8.6	7.0	8.4 }
Total investment..........	100.0	100.0	100.0	100.0	100.0	100.0	100.0	100.0	100.0	100.0	100.0

The lag in dividend payments can be attributed to two main factors. First, much of the nonresident investment has been made to develop new resource-based industries without expectation of immediate return on the investment. Also there has been a marked slowdown in demand for Canadian resource materials since 1957, reflecting both the development of alternative sources of supply in other areas and the slower rate of economic expansion in the United States.

Breakdowns by industry of investment in capital stock and other corporate assets of Canadian companies by U.S. investors and other nonresidents is not available. The main areas of U.S. interest in recent years, however, are indicated in Table 22 which shows the net inflows of U.S. capital for direct investment in Canada (gross inflows less return of capital).

36

TABLE 22

Net U.S. Capital Inflow for Direct Investment in Canada by Industry

	1955	1956	1957	1958	1959	1960	1955	1956	1957	1958	1959	1960
	(Millions of dollars)						(Percent)					
Petroleum and natural gas......	193	221	236	209	165	169	63.1	54.4	60.5	69.0	38.9	38.7
Mining............	60	44	62	71	107	206	19.6	10.8	15.9	23.4	25.2	47.1
Pulp and Paper.....	−5	37	33	−8	−6	20	−1.6	9.2	8.5	−2.6	−1.4	4.6
Manufacturing.....	24	73	45	33	105	4	7.8	18.0	11.5	10.9	24.8	0.9
Other.............	34	31	14	−2	53	38	11.1	7.6	3.6	−0.7	12.5	8.7
Total.........	*306*	*406*	*390*	*303*	*424*	*437*	*100.0*	*100.0*	*100.0*	*100.0*	*100.0*	*100.0*

While development of resource industries has absorbed roughly three quarters of nonresident investment over the past decade, manufacturing has provided over one half of total dividend payments over this period, as illustrated in Tables 23 and 24.

TABLE 23

Industrial Distribution of Canadian Dividend Payments to Nonresidents, Selected Years

(Millions of Dollars)

	All Nonresidents			U.S. Residents		
	1950	1958	1960	1950	1958	1960
Total manufacturing.................	230	187	192	210	160	162
Nonmanufacturing...................	128	244	222	105	187	166
Petroleum and natural gas..........	13	43	57	13	40	54
Mining and smelting..............	57	84	59	51	73	48
Utilities.........................	24	39	32	14	17	17
Other...........................	34	78	74	28	57	47
Combined total[1].....................	*366*	*431*	*414*	*322*	*347*	*328*

[1] Includes small unclassified items.

TABLE 24

Percentage Industrial Distribution of Canadian Dividend Payments to Nonresidents, Selected Years

(Percent)

	All Nonresidents			U.S. Residents		
	1950	1958	1960	1950	1958	1960
Total manufacturing.................	62.8	43.3	46.4	65.2	46.1	49.4
Nonmanufacturing...................	35.0	56.7	53.6	32.7	53.9	50.6
Petroleum and natural gas..........	3.5	10.0	13.8	4.0	11.5	16.5
Mining and smelting..............	15.6	19.4	14.3	15.8	21.1	14.6
Utilities.........................	6.5	9.0	7.7	4.3	4.9	5.2
Other...........................	9.4	18.3	17.9	8.7	16.4	14.3
Combined total[1].....................	*100.0*	*100.0*	*100.0*	*100.0*	*100.0*	*100.0*

[1] Percentages for 1950 do not add to 100 due to inclusion of small unclassified items.

The second main factor contributing to the lag in dividend payments, as compared with the growth of nonresident ownership of capital stock and other assets of Canadian companies, has been the retention in Canada of a considerable part of the earnings of these companies. For example, from 1951 to 1960 inclusive, estimated total return on foreign direct investment in Canada amounted to $6.6 billion of which $2.9 billion was remitted after allowance for withholding tax—while $3.4 billion, or 52 percent of total earnings, was retained as undistributed profits. Figures showing retained earnings arising from nonresident portfolio investment in Canada are not available. It is reasonable to assume, however, that the ratio of retention to total earnings has approximated the average for all companies in Canada which, between 1952 and 1960, retained about half of earnings. Consequently, the total of retained earnings on nonresident investment in capital stock of Canadian companies probably is considerably in excess of the figure shown above. Canada's balance of payments does not reflect the accrual to non-residents of these undistributed earnings, an important source of corporate financing and a significant factor in the rapid growth of the equity of non-residents in Canadian industry and commerce. Retained earnings, therefore, are tantamount to the introduction of additional capital from abroad.

Decisions with respect to the transfer or retention of earnings are presumably influenced primarily by the need for funds. Unless there are immediate and pressing requirements for funds, conditions in the exchange and money markets assume importance. The corporation's over-all tax position is also a determinant—particularly in the subsidiary-parent relationship, typical of direct investment, as opposed to the public company whose profit distributions represent a financial disposition of resources and for whose shareholders the relatively stable dividend rate generally has attraction.

The ability to make an actual income payment is closely related to the liquidity of the company. Generally, apart from the raising or return of capital, changes in liquidity reflect not only profits but also cash flows to the company arising from noncash charges less the amounts used for capital expenditures and inventory changes. Given a high level of cash flows, it is possible for a moderate decline in profits after taxation to be more than compensated for by reductions in capital expenditures, and for moderating economic activity to give rise, under certain conditions, to larger amounts of funds being available for transfer abroad.

Another aspect of significance is the flexibility open to companies to use available excess funds to pay off debts rather than to transfer earnings, particularly in the case where the holder of equity is also the holder of debt. The economic distinction between the payment of a dividend and the repayment of debt, with simultaneous growth in surplus, is of limited significance. The extent to which this practice can occur is restricted, of course, by the amount of capital originally supplied in the nominal form of debt. Many motives may lie behind the choice of the original capital structure and the subsequent accounting treatment for transfer of funds. Probably most lie in the fields of administrative regulation, legal and tax considerations, and accounting effects. The growing volume of retained earnings being accumulated by nonresident-owned companies is regarded by some as a source of potential weakness in Canada's balance of payments position. Serious concern on this score, however, does not appear to be justified, especially since only a small percentage of retained earnings is typically held in liquid form, with the great bulk of such earnings being invested in inventory and various forms of fixed assets. The result is that retained earnings are not readily available for sudden withdrawal.

6

Business Services and
Other Transactions

While the Dominion Bureau of Statistics treats business services and other transactions with its survey of Miscellaneous Current Transactions in its annual report on the Canadian Balance of International Payments, this study attempts to deal with these separately because of the very important role of such transactions in Canada's non-merchandise payments position. Apart from 1946, statistical breakdowns are not available until 1952. Consequently, the discussion of figures in this chapter relates only to the years subsequent to 1951.

The specific items included in this category of transactions embrace a wide spectrum of activities but broadly may be classified as business, professional, and personal services. In the past, a large part of "other transactions" consisted of payments by railways for special services, and insurance transactions such as the remittance of premiums, and the payment of claims and contributions toward head office expenses. Some of the largest components of business services, particularly on the payment side, are transactions between nonresident head offices and their branches, subsidiaries or other direct affiliates in Canada. Large elements of the cost of initial investment represent fees for such services as architectural design, engineering, consulting, and other assistance in industrial techniques and processes. In some cases, they represent the rental of special equipment and machinery. Subsequently, when operations commence, appreciable fees are usually

41

charged for royalties, management, and the apportionment of nonresident head-office expenses, such as advertising, accounting, and research. These "operational" payments have risen proportionately from about one fourth of business services in 1952 to over two fifths currently, and totaled nearly $155 million in 1961.

There is also a wide variety of payments and receipts for services between unaffiliated enterprises and persons in Canada and abroad for the growing exchange of commercial, financial, and professional services, all of which form an integral part of Canada's business life. Included are items such as licensing fees for manufacturing patents, processes and trademarks, franchises, authors' and composers' royalties, copyrights, royalties for master recordings, syndicated features and cartoons, commissions and fees for legal, accounting, and management services, and for other consulting and professional services. Rentals of foreign films, and payment for television programming, expenditures of international airlines and other transportation payments not embodied in freight and shipping account are some additional examples of importance included among business service transactions. Finally, also covered in this account are estimates of earnings of migrant labour and international commuters, remittances for international sweepstakes, and trade union transfers.

Unfortunately for purposes of analysis, dollar figures for the separate types of business service payments are not published. It is expected that returns which will be filed in the future under the authority of the recently enacted disclosure bill affecting corporations and labour unions will help fill this gap in information. It is believed that the most important category in terms of dollar amounts is head-office expenses. This category includes all administrative charges by foreign parents to branches, subsidiaries or affiliates. Since it is known that many flat or percentage charge arrangements include not only administrative but also engineering, research, marketing and other types of services, that are not specified as such, the designation "head-office expenses" is not too meaningful.

Although receipts on business services between 1952 and 1962 increased at almost the same annual rate as payments—5.5 percent for receipts, compared with 5.75 percent for payments—payments have been approximately twice as large, with the result that the spread between the two has become wider almost every year. Since 1953, for example, deficits on this item increased steadily from a low point of $129 million in that year to $246 million in 1962. Though the deficit arising from business services has grown steadily, it has grown slowly compared with deficits incurred from interest and dividend or miscellaneous payments, and accounted in 1962 for 24.5 percent of the total deficit on non-merchandise transactions compared with 42 percent in 1952.

Since 1952, around 73 percent of receipts and 86 percent of payments have been derived from transactions with the United States. Moreover, since 1952, over 98 percent of Canada's accumulated deficits on this item have arisen from transactions with the United States. Transactions with the rest of the world are growing, however, and while they still remain of minor significance, they have become relatively more important in recent years. Receipts from the United States as a percentage of total receipts have declined from a peak of 75 percent in 1955 to slightly under 70 percent in 1961, while payments to the United States have fallen from 91 percent of total payments in 1952 to less than 84 percent in 1961. These trends reflect in part increasing Canadian investment overseas and the growth of British and European investment in Canada in recent years. Between 1952 and 1961, the United Kingdom accounted for somewhat more than half of all transactions with overseas countries. Britain's receipts from Canada, however, have closely approximated payments to that country and the account has usually been in balance. Small deficits in such transactions have occurred with other overseas countries every year, ranging between $1 million and $6 million per annum.

The steady growth of business and personal transactions included under the Business Service category is the result of two main trends: the growing business, scientific, cultural, and military links between Canada and the United States; the continuing heavy American investment in Canada's economic development throughout the whole range of business activity, from resource exploration to highly specialized professional consulting services.

In the majority of instances, the investment of capital has involved foreign control of the company or facility. Foreign control usually has meant that decisions to employ specialized engineering, marketing, advertising, economic, legal, architectural and other professional skills were made in the United States within a framework of corporate policy and tested experience for using U.S. sources of these skills. Against this background, and because of the high quality and ready availability of these skills in the United States and the United Kingdom, the development of Canadian talent and facilities in these specialized fields has without doubt been inhibited.

While charges relating to the development of Canada's primary resources still account for an important portion of Canada's total payments on business services and other transactions, in more recent years an increasing percentage has arisen in connection with the establishment and operation of nonresident owned or controlled manufacturing facilities. This percentage is currently estimated at 60 percent. In the field of research, for example, a significant proportion of expenditures on industrial research and development are made to companies outside Canada.

Estimates in the Dominion Bureau of Statistics reports on *Industrial Research-Development Expenditures in Canada* indicate that of total research expenditures made by the reporting companies in 1955, 1957 and 1959, between 13 and 18 percent was made in other countries. There are strong reasons to suggest that these figures tend to understate the true extent of dependence on non-Canadian research sources. Compared with the United States and Britain, for example, research actually performed in Canada, including government, industry, universities and others, is on a much smaller scale, relatively. For example, in 1959, the ratio of research and development expenditures made in Canada to gross national product was 0.72 percent compared with 2.58 percent in the United States and 2.11 percent in the United Kingdom in 1958/59.[1]

The diversity of contractual agreements makes it difficult to generalize on the major factors that influence the trend or absolute level of such payments. Very few cases have been found where charges for business services are related to fluctuations in net profits. On the other hand, a large number of arrangements, perhaps the majority, tie the business service charge to a percentage of gross sales. Many companies have a fixed charge, but for a minority, particularly young subsidiaries, service payments are held to a minimum to allow an earnings build-up for future expansion. In general, however, it can be said that business service payments are tied to some measure of business activity, though not the extreme cyclical one of gross profits.

Table 25 compares annual figures for industrial production with an index of business service payments to the United States. While annual figures provide an unsatisfactory basis for appraising cyclical influences, even within this limitation, it is evident that strong expansions in industrial production have been accompanied, or shortly followed, by large increases in business service payments.

TABLE 25

Canadian Industrial Production and Business Service Payments to the United States

(Indexes, 1952=100)

	Canadian Index of Industrial Production	Index of Business Service Payments to the United States
1952............	100	100
1953............	106.8	98.2
1954............	106.3	104.0
1955............	117.7	109.4
1956............	128.1	122.8
1957............	128.5	127.7
1958............	127.7	130.8
1959............	137.4	132.6
1960............	138.5	136.6
1961............	143.0	148.7
1962............	154.1	161.1

It has been suggested that tax considerations have at times influenced the parent company charge for business services to their subsidiaries, branches or affiliates. On the few occasions when the Canadian corporate tax rate has exceeded the U.S. rate, there has been an incentive to charge the subsidiary company with a full burden of business service charges in order to minimize the exposure to taxes in a relatively high tax area. If the United States cor-

---

[1] See 44th *Annual Report* of the National Research Council of Canada, 1960-61.

porate tax rate were to decline relative to the Canadian rate this tendency would undoubtedly reappear, with the effect of increasing the deficit arising from business services.

On balance, it is not believed that tax considerations have been a prime determinant of the level of business service payments. There is some reason to believe, however, that in the past, Canadian tax authorities have been more lenient than American authorities in approving scales of payments, contractual or otherwise, as legitimate expenses for tax purposes.

There appears to be a trend, particularly in the case of manufacturing, commercial, and retailing subsidiaries, for parent company charges for administrative and technical help to be levied increasingly at realistic rates.

Payments arising from the close cultural, recreational, and educational ties between Canada and the United States have been one of the fastest growing segments of service payments. In particular, payments for advertising, television programs, entertainment, and publishing have expanded sharply in recent years under the stimulus of rising personal incomes and increased leisure time. Canadian resources in these areas are increasing rather slowly, and one can anticipate a long period of increasing deficits from such activities.

It is interesting to draw attention to one particular form of payment as an indication of the diversity of activities covered in this section and the dollar amounts involved. It is privately estimated that net payments outside the country—mainly to Europe—for lottery tickets total around $50 million (that is, payments for lottery tickets in excess of winnings), although the official estimate is much lower.

Looking to the future, it is difficult to see any basic causes for any abrupt change in the circumstances affecting the present pattern of business service payments. Contractual arrangements and corporate habits are not quickly broken. It is possible, however, to foresee gradual development of Canadian skills and service facilities under the impact of a growing economy, a higher retention (or perhaps even repatriation) of highly educated and trained Canadian specialists, a greater awareness by foreign companies of Canadian facilities, and some prodding by government in this direction, leading to the growing use of such Canadian facilities by both foreign and domestic corporations, institutions, and individuals. There is already evidence to suggest that such a trend is under way.

7

Freight and Shipping

Transactions relating to freight and shipping comprise receipts and payments for international transportation services. The principal Canadian payments are those made by Canadian importers for services performed by foreign ships, railways, trucks, pipelines or aircraft carrying imports to Canada. Also included are expenditures to service Canadian ships in foreign ports and transportation outlays in the United States in moving Canadian goods from one part of Canada to another partially by U.S. facilities, and for time charter hire of foreign ships by Canadians. The principal receipts are the earnings of Canadian carriers transporting exports, and the earnings of Canadian railways from the carriage of goods between foreign points via Canada. Receipts from expenditures in Canada arising from the operation of nonresident owned railways in Canada and the earnings of Canadian ships operating between foreign ports are both included in this account. Transportation expenses of travelers are included in travel account, including both payments to foreign carriers transporting Canadian travelers and receipts from Canadian carriers transporting foreigners.

Since Canadian import valuations exclude the cost of freight and other services relating to the transportation of merchandise from the country of purchase to the Canadian border or port of entry, such costs are included in freight and shipping account whenever these services are supplied by nonresidents. Similarly, because Canadian exports are generally valued at the point of shipment in Canada, it is necessary to include in the freight account the earnings of Canadian carriers from the carriage of Canadian exports to the Canadian border.

The value of freight and shipping transactions is determined primarily by the volume of exports and imports, the level of transportation rates (after exchange conversions), and the availability of domestic transportation carriers. Growing trade volume and successive increases in freight rates have increased both Canada's receipts and payments over the postwar period. In general, Canada's balance on freight and shipping account has been influenced by the predominant direction and changing composition of trade and by the varying levels of activity of Canada's merchant fleet.

Since 1946, transactions relating to freight and shipping account have been another category of non-merchandise transactions in which Canada's net payments balance with the United States has been largely responsible for the deficit on that item. In fact, whereas Canada has always experienced deficits on freight and shipping account with the United States (with the exception of 1959), it has customarily earned surpluses both with the United Kingdom and with other overseas countries as a group.

TABLE 26
Canada's Balances on Freight and Shipping Account
(Millions of Dollars)

	1950	1951	1952	1953	1954	1955	1956	1957	1958	1959	1960	1961	1962
With the United States	−83	−112	−128	−132	−92	−84	−128	−129	−88	−98	−104	−103	−107e
With the United Kingdom....	+25	+ 48	+ 63	+ 37	+34	+48	+ 39	+ 26	+14	− 5	+ 4	+ 7	n.a.
With other countries....	+41	+ 61	+ 73	+ 39	+15	+19	+ 44	+ 33	+15	− 2	+ 9	+ 14	n.a.
Total......	−17	− 3	+ 8	− 56	−43	−17	− 45	− 70	−59	−105	− 91	− 82	−90

e Estimated.
n.a. Not available.

In the period from 1946 to 1949, the surpluses with all overseas countries taken together were relatively large and considerably in excess of the net payments to the United States. The result was that Canada enjoyed an over-all favourable balance on these transactions amounting to about $50 million a year ($92 million in 1946). Since 1949, the surpluses with overseas countries have been smaller while the deficits with the United States continued to run between $80 million and $130 million a year, the over-all effect being that during the past decade Canada has incurred deficits on freight and shipping account in every year except 1952.

The deficit with the United States arises principally from the consistent and large deficit on commodity trade. The surpluses earned from transactions with overseas countries have been on a declining trend in recent years, falling from $83 million in 1956 to a deficit of $7 million in 1959 (although with surpluses reappearing in 1960 and 1961).

An important factor contributing to Canada's large receipts from freight and shipping immediately following World War II was the substantial increase in the number and tonnage of Canadian owned and operated merchant ships as a result of the construction of 398 such vessels during the war. Following the end of hostilities, of the 258 dry-cargo ships owned by the government, 150 were sold to private Canadian operators. Due to the high freight rates prevailing at the time—as a consequence of the wartime disruption of world

TABLE 27

Canadian Merchant Fleet

(Ships over 1,000 gross tons, as at March 31)

Ocean-going Ships in Foreign Trade	1947[1]	1952	1953	1954	1955	1956	1957	1960	1961	1962
Number of ships	153	77	65	57	27	25	26	16	17	4
Gross tons	982,869	530,000	442,000	324,031	204,000	183,336	186,165	136,177	159,655	59,124
Canadian-owned Ships under U.K. registry										
Number of ships	80	97	96	101	103	99	83	35	27	24
Gross tons	560,000	693,221	686,672	710,219	723,967	709,171	604,119	252,641	190,380	166,163

[1] Ships over 1,600 gross tons (Hansard, 1947, vol. V, p. 4203).
Source: *Annual Reports* of the Canadian Maritime Commission.

TABLE 28

Flag Participation in the Carriage of Canada's Overseas Trade, Dry Cargo Only

(Trade with or via the United States excluded)

	1947	1948	1949	1950	1951	1952	1953	1954	1955	1956	1957	1958	1959	1960
Total dry cargo exported and imported (mils. of tons[1])	16.3	15.2	17.0	15.3	21.6	25.8	24.8	23.1	29.9	30.1	29.1	27.1	29.5	33.1
% Carried in:						(Percentage Distribution)								
Canadian flag ships	20.2	17.9	13.6	9.9	7.9	6.4	4.3	2.1	2.4	1.4	1.0	0.2	0.03	0.2
U.K. flag ships	45.2	46.3	43.1	48.8	40.6	35.4	34.0	33.8	29.2	31.3	30.0	32.2	29.1	30.3
Norwegian flag ships	3.4	9.3	11.9	11.5	10.2	12.4	13.5	15.1	13.3	13.7	15.4	15.8	19.8	19.6
Other flag ships	31.2	26.5	31.4	29.8	41.3	45.8	48.2	49.0	55.1	53.6	53.6	51.8	51.1	49.9
Total	100%	100%	100%	100%	100%	100%	100%	100%	100%	100%	100%	100%	100%	100%

[1] 1 ton = 2,000 lbs.

49

shipping—these vessels were operated profitably in 1946 and 1947, and a relatively large proportion of Canadian overseas trade was carried in Canadian ships. In 1948, however, the situation became less favourable for Canadian operators as other maritime nations began to take delivery of new vessels which were more modern than Canadian merchant ships. The problems of Canadian operators were intensified by the currency devaluations of 1949, relatively high wage rates for seamen, and the measures adopted by many governments to control the outflow of dollars. The latter actions severely inhibited expenditures by overseas countries on freight and shipping facilities owned by dollar-area countries. Canadian shipowners found they could not compete with overseas flags and sold many of their hulls in 1948 and 1949 and placed many of the remainder under British registration and management in 1950. While profits derived from the operation of the latter have reverted to the Canadian owners, Canada's freight and shipping balances have, of course, not benefitted from the much larger gross revenues derived from the operation of these vessels. The decline of Canada's ocean-going merchant fleet is shown in Table 27.

The decline in the importance of Canada's ocean-going merchant fleet as a carrier of Canada's overseas trade is shown dramatically in the figures, provided by the Fifteenth Report of the Canadian Maritime Commission, which are reproduced in Table 28.

As might be expected, Canada's increasing reliance upon nonresident owned shipping facilities for the transportation of its overseas trade has been an important reason for the decline in the size of the surpluses earned on freight and shipping account with Britain and other overseas countries. For example, despite the growth of overseas exports, ocean freight receipts from the carriage of these exports by Canadian vessels declined from $65 million in 1956 to $60 million in 1961. Over the same period, however, payments arising from ocean-shipping charges on the carriage of imports from overseas countries by non-Canadian shipping rose from $65 million to $124 million. Table 29 shows the change in Canada's position with overseas countries in respect to receipts and payments arising from all forms of ocean-shipping charges. These not only include ocean freight on imports and exports, but also receipts and payments derived from time charters, as well as expenditures of foreign ships in Canada and Canadian ships in foreign countries.

TABLE 29

Canada's Receipts and Payments arising from the Transportation of Ocean Freight between Canada and Overseas Countries
(Millions of Dollars)

	Receipts			Payments			Balance		
	1951	1956	1961	1951	1956	1961	1951	1956	1961
United Kingdom	61	67	61	43	59	93	+18	+8	−32
Other countries	51	87	88	35	92	142	+16	−5	−54
All overseas countries	112	154	149	78	151	235	+34	+3	−86

Apart from the decline and stagnation of the Canadian merchant fleet, the growing importance of nonresident owned ocean shipping as a carrier of Canadian trade reflects the increasing percentage of imports coming from overseas countries as shown in Table 30. Between 1951 and 1962, imports from overseas countries grew at a rate of slightly over 4 percent per annum, while payments for ocean freight charges on these imports increased at a rate of over 10 percent per annum.

TABLE 30

Merchandise Imports from Overseas Countries as a Percentage of Total Canadian Merchandise Imports

Imports from	1951	1952	1953	1954	1955	1956	1957	1958	1959	1960	1961	1962
United Kingdom.....	10.2	9.1	11.0	10.0	8.9	8.9	9.5	10.6	10.8	11.0	10.7	9.3
Other overseas countries	20.4	17.7	16.7	18.5	18.8	18.9	19.9	21.4	22.2	22.0	22.3	22.8
All countries except the United States........	20.6	26.8	27.7	28.5	27.7	27.8	29.4	32.0	33.0	33.0	33.0	32.1

While the figures for the years between 1956 and 1961 are not available, it is evident that Canada experienced deficits with overseas countries on ocean-shipping transactions during most of those years. Consequently, Canada's over-all surplus position on freight and shipping transactions with these countries since 1956 is attributable to receipts from inland freight on exports destined for abroad, amounting to $107 million in 1961 compared with $80 million in 1956, against which no offsetting payments are involved.

A small part of Canada's trade with the United States is carried by ocean-going ships, and receipts and payments arising from these services constitute but a small part of total freight and shipping account with that country. While ocean freight receipts on exports to the United States have climbed from $5 million in 1951 to $23 million in 1961, receipts from the carriage of U.S. cargoes between foreign ports and from time charter arrangements declined from $17 million in 1951 to $6 million in 1961. As a result, total ocean freight receipts from the United States have experienced little growth from $22 million to $29 million over the ten-year period. Payments to the United States for ocean freight on imports have been equally small and stable, rising from $33 million in 1951 to $40 million in 1961.

Expenditures of U.S. ships in Canada have almost disappeared amounting to only $2 million in 1961, compared with $6 million in 1951. Payments attributable to expenditures of Canadian vessels in American ports and to time charter arrangements with U.S. operators have declined from $25 million in 1951 to $19 million in 1961.

With the decline in the size of Canada's ocean-going merchant fleet, the proportion of Canada's total freight and shipping receipts derived from the earnings of Canada's merchant fleet has fallen substantially from around 40 percent in 1946 to 23 percent in 1960 and 1961, with occasional interruptions in this trend during such periods as the Korean War and the Suez Crisis. At the same time, the proportion of freight and shipping payments attributable to the expenses of Canadian vessels in foreign ports and to time charter payments has not changed appreciably since 1946, running normally between 18 and 23 percent, but in excess of 20 percent since 1956. It may be supposed that expenses of Canadian ships abroad have become relatively less significant but to the same extent that time charter payments have become relatively more important.

The expansion of Canada's trade with overseas countries since the war has been reflected in a remarkable upsurge in the ratio of shipping payments on ocean-borne imports to total freight and shipping payments, the ratio having risen from a little less than 4 percent in 1946 to almost 30 percent in 1960 and 1961. Despite the increased activity of nonresident owned shipping in Canadian ports, however, the proportion of freight and shipping receipts derived from the expenditures of these vessels in Canada has varied considerably, ranging between about 10 and 15 percent, and has not been characterized by any trend.

In summary, receipts from all charges from ocean-shipping in relation to total freight and shipping receipts are less important than they were in the early postwar years when Canada's merchant fleet was a significant factor in the carriage of the country's export trade. The proportion of total freight and shipping receipts derived from the revenues of Canadian-operated ships and the expenditures of foreign ships in Canadian ports fell from over 50 percent in 1946 and 1947, to 38 percent in 1950, and has fluctuated at between 33 and 40 percent since then. On the other side, however, the proportion of freight and shipping payments attributable to ocean freight payments on imports, together with the expenditures of Canadian ships abroad and time charter payments, has risen steadily from 32 percent in 1946 to over 50 percent in 1960 and 1961.

In terms of the size of the transactions involved, the earnings of Canadian railways and other transportation agencies from the carriage of Canada's exports from their point of shipment in Canada to the Canadian border or seaport constitute a source of receipts even more important than ocean-shipping. Such earnings from individual export components obviously are subject to the influence of changes in the structure of domestic freight rates, and in the composition of Canada's export trade and of new developments or improvements in the internal transportation system. Nevertheless, as Table 31 indicates, over the postwar period the total of such receipts has shown a remarkably consistent relationship to the total value of exports.

Receipts from inland freight on exports consist primarily of freight charges imposed for the transportation of goods by rail to the Canadian border or an ocean port or from the movement of goods by ship in the inland water system. Other receipts are derived from the movement of commodities by pipeline, truck, and aircraft, and also the water shipment of iron ore from the Quebec North Shore. Despite the growth of exports over the past decade, related inland freight receipts have not experienced a similar trend. While such receipts advanced from $116 million in 1946 to $201 million in 1952, after running at a somewhat lower level from 1953 to 1955, they have hovered at around the $200 million level in subsequent years. Consequently, as Table

31 shows, since the early 1950s there has been a tendency for the "inland freight on exports" ratio to decline.

On the other hand, this declining tendency generally has been matched by a comparable increase in the "other receipts" ratio. Until 1955, other receipts had been a very minor item, ranging normally between $3 million and $8 million a year. In 1955, however, they jumped to $21 million and subsequently increased to $47 million in 1961. These trends appear to be the effect, in part, of changes in the composition of the country's export trade and of the development of new export resources which are most economically or easily transported by means other than rail. The movement of crude oil by pipeline, and of iron ore from Quebec's North Shore are cases in point. The increased use of trucking and air freight probably is another important factor. In more recent years, these trends have been affected by the opening of the St. Lawrence Seaway which has reduced the distance, and therefore the inland freight receipts, required to carry export commodities by rail from their point of origin to lake or ocean-going shipping.

Canada's non-merchandise payments for inland rail freight and other inland transportation services concerns imports from the United States alone. An examination of these payments reveals that in the postwar period there has been a marked decline in the ratio of payments for inland rail freight to the value of imports from the United States—a decline that is far more pronounced than that experienced in the comparable ratio of inland freight receipts to total Canadian exports.

Such payments result from freight charged by U.S. railways on goods transported from Mexico and the United States to the Canadian border or to lake and river ports where they can be transshipped by vessel. For many years such payments for inland freight on U.S. imports were the most important part of Canada's total payments on freight and shipping and were considerably in excess of gross payments on ocean shipping. Since 1955, however, when they reached a postwar peak of $221 million, these payments have declined sharply to $153 million in 1960 (the lowest point in a decade), and have become considerably less important than payments on ocean shipping. An important element in this trend has been the decline of coal imports from the United States, which fell from around $185 million in 1950 and 1951 to $91 million in 1960. Freight payments on coal imports arriving by rail have been declining for a decade from a postwar high of $40 million in 1950 to a low of $8 million in 1960. While freight payments on coal imports arriving by vessel remained fairly stable over much of the 1950s at between $40 million and $50 million a year, they have been running at a lower level of between $34 million and $35 million a year since 1958. The decline in coal imports largely reflects increasing competition from oil and gas for many industrial and domestic uses. Oil imports into Canada arrive by ship or pipeline, a much cheaper form of transportation than rail. Payments for rail freight on other imports from the United States have not experienced as distinct a declining trend as have similar payments for coal

53

imports. In fact, from 1946 to 1956, the trend was generally upward with payments reaching a peak of $143 million in 1956. Since then annual payments have declined to a level of $110 million in 1960.

Declining payments for inland rail freight on imports from the United States in spite of the growing volume of such imports, have been offset to a considerable extent by rising payments for trucking and air freight service as well as pipelines. The substantial rise in the miscellaneous payments component of the freight and shipping account reflects the trend toward increased use of air and road transport from the United States in recent years. The growth of these payments has been moving at a relatively faster pace than has the growth of imports from the United States.

Consequently, the ratio of miscellaneous payments to the value of imports from the United States has tended to rise since the late 1940s. The combination of the rail freight ratio and the miscellaneous payments ratio indicates a gradual decline in Canada's payments for freight on a large part of this country's imports from the United States in relation to the growth of these imports. The growth of relatively cheaper forms of transportation appears to have been an important factor contributing to this trend. Furthermore, the outlook is promising for a continuation of this trend, one which is favourable to Canada's balance of payments.

Apart from shipping receipts and inland freight on exports, the transportation category includes in-transit revenues and certain other receipts. In-transit revenues include earnings of Canadian railways carrying goods through parts of Canada between two points in the United States. In addition, certain international credits are derived from expenditures in Canada arising out of in-transit traffic across southwestern Ontario on U.S. owned or operated railways. These receipts arise mainly from outlays for operations in Canada and include wages to Canadian employees, rentals, taxes and so forth. In-transit revenues have been fairly stable over the postwar period but have experienced moderate growth over the past decade from $28 million in 1950 to $40 million in 1959 and $38 million in 1960. Other receipts were a very minor item until 1955, ranging normally between $3 million and $8 million a year. In 1955, they jumped to $21 million and increased from that level to $41 million in 1957 and $39 million in 1959 and 1960.

The increasing dependence of Canada's overseas trade upon foreign shipping accounts, in part at least, for the change in the distribution of Canada's payments on freight and shipping account which has become noticeable since 1953. Prior to and including 1953, the United States received between 76 and 80 percent of Canada's total freight and shipping payments in each year, while the U.K. share fluctuated between 11 and 15 percent and that of all other countries between 8 and 11 percent. Since 1953, however, the U.S. share has declined almost every year to about 61 percent in 1960. The U.K. share, on the other hand, has increased steadily from 11 percent in 1953 to close to 17 percent in 1960, and the share of all other countries from about 10 percent in 1953 to over 22 percent in 1960. This growing

TABLE 31

Ratio of Receipts derived from Inland Freight on Exports and other Receipts to Total Canadian Exports

(Percent)

	1946	1947	1948	1949	1950	1951	1952	1953	1954	1955	1956	1957	1958	1959	1960	1961
Inland freight on exports......	4.8	4.4	4.9	4.7	4.5	4.5	4.6	3.9	4.0	4.3	4.2	4.0	3.9	3.9	3.8	3.8
Other receipts................	0.1	0.2	0.2	0.1	0.2	0.1	0.2	0.1	0.2	0.5	0.7	0.8	0.6	0.8	0.7	0.8
Combined....................	4.9	4.6	5.1	4.8	4.7	4.6	4.8	4.0	4.2	4.8	4.9	4.8	4.5	4.7	4.5	4.6

TABLE 32

Ratio of Canadian Miscellaneous Payments and Payments for Inland Rail Freight in the United States on Imports to Total Canadian Imports from the United States

(Percent)

	1946	1947	1948	1949	1950	1951	1952	1953	1954	1955	1956	1957	1958	1959	1960	1961
Rail freight ratio.............	9.1	8.4	9.1	7.4	8.3	6.5	7.0	6.4	6.2	5.5	5.5	5.4	4.7	4.6	4.1	3.7
Miscellaneous payments ratio..	1.7	1.2	1.0	1.0	1.1	1.2	1.4	1.4	1.8	1.9	1.8	2.2	2.6	2.8	2.9	3.4
Combined ratio...............	10.8	9.6	10.1	8.4	9.4	7.7	8.4	7.8	8.0	7.4	7.3	7.6	7.3	7.4	7.0	7.1

importance of overseas countries is also due in part to their increasing role as exporters to Canada.

The geographical distribution of Canada's receipts on freight and shipping account has also experienced some shifts. The proportion of receipts derived from the United Kingdom has declined steadily while in recent years receipts from other overseas countries and the United States have increased. Overseas countries (excluding the United Kingdom) currently account for roughly 30 percent of total receipts compared with less than 23 percent in 1954, while the U.S. share has risen from around 36 percent in the early postwar years to 53 percent currently.

These trends reflect both the decline in Canadian owned merchant shipping and the increase in exports to overseas countries and the United States.

Looking to the future there is reason to be mildly optimistic that the deficit on freight and shipping charges can be reduced. The current drive to expand exports in an effort to reduce Canada's large current account payments deficit will undoubtedly meet with some success, and past experience has established a rough correlation between the balance on freight and shipping account and merchandise trade. Over time, Canada's exports should include a rising proportion of more highly processed goods on which transport charges are higher, and this will tend to increase the country's transportation earnings—although the shorter average hauls associated with such products and cost reducing innovations in transportation may tend to slow any such increase. On the other hand, increasing self-sufficiency in such items as oil, steel, and other basic commodities will reduce heavy transportation payments now associated with the import of these goods. The loss in receipts arising from the virtual disappearance of Canada's ocean-going merchant fleet has already been absorbed. On the credit side will be a growing volume of receipts from the expected growth of air freight, trucking, pipelines, and Canadian inland shipping stimulated by the St. Lawrence Seaway.

8

Inheritances and Migrant Funds[1]

Separate figures are not published for inheritances and migrant funds. By far the largest portion of the combined total consists of migrant funds, both for receipts and payments. Immigrant funds (receipts) ranged from about 80 percent of total receipts in 1952 to almost 85 percent in 1957, the year of peak postwar immigration, but have subsequently declined to about 67 percent in 1961. Emigrant funds (payments) have risen over the past decade from about 70 percent of total payments to 80 percent currently.

Inheritances have been estimated to have increased moderately but steadily in the past decade, on the assumption that this pattern of behaviour, characteristic of this item for a number of years prior to 1952, has continued. Thus, although factors influencing trends for each of these items differ, the discussion centers principally on those that help explain fluctuations in

---

[1]*Inheritances*—Funds transferred to Canadians arising from a foreign inheritance and funds transferred from Canadians to foreigners as a result of a Canadian inheritance.

Migrant funds—an inclusive term used to describe both funds brought to Canada by immigrants at the time of first arrival (immigrant funds) and funds taken out of Canada by emigrants at the time of departure (emigrant funds). The account includes immigrant funds transferred subsequent to arrival if specific arrangements for such transfer were made at the time of immigration. Otherwise subsequent remittances of earnings by immigrants or emigrants to their homeland are not included in this figure but recorded as personal remittances under the miscellaneous section of the balance of payment account. Goods and chattels are not included in the calculation of migrant funds.

57

migrant funds. When one compares the trend of migrant funds with that of immigration, a rough correlation is found, as might be expected.

Since the end of World War II, Canada has absorbed slightly in excess of 2 million immigrants from other countries. Offsetting this gain has been substantial emigration, which to the United States alone, has accounted for a loss of more than 500,000 during the same period. A further attrition of around 130,000 resulted from emigration to the United Kingdom. Furthermore, the United Nations Demographic Year Book indicates that between 1950 and 1958 at least 42,000 people emigrated from Canada to Continental Europe and 21,300 to all remaining countries.

The flow of immigrants to Canada has had an irregular pattern over the past 15 years but between 1951 and 1960 consistently exceeded 100,000 a year. From 1951 to 1955, there was a declining trend and immigration fell from an annual rate of 194,000 to 110,000. The inflow jumped sharply in 1956 to 165,000 and again in 1957 to a postwar peak of 282,000. Subsequently, however, the downward trend reappeared and the inflow of 71,689 immigrants in 1961 represented the lowest level since 1947. A moderate increase to 74,600 occurred in 1962.

It is interesting to note that on three occasions since the war, abnormally large increases in immigration occurred in periods of acute international tension. In 1948, for example, immigration to Canada increased by almost 50 percent to over 125,000 because of the widespread fear of war, generated in Continental Europe by the collapse of attempts to place atomic weapons under international control, the absorption of Czechoslovakia into the Soviet sphere of influence, and the crisis associated with the Berlin Blockade. Immigration declined in 1949 and 1950, principally because of a severe decline in the number of arrivals from the United Kingdom as a result of financial restrictions imposed by that country to solve the exchange crisis which arose at that time. In 1951, however, immigration soared by 121,000 to over 194,000 and it is probably more than coincidence that this occurred shortly after the Chinese intervention in the Korean War the previous November. The general anxiety and disillusionment that permeated Europe as a result of the Hungarian rebellion and the Suez Crisis in 1956 clearly had considerable impact upon immigration to Canada which experienced another phase of exceptionally large immigration. Arrivals to Canada totaled 165,000 in 1956 and 282,000 in 1957 compared with 110,000 in 1955. Since 1958, rapidly expanding business activity in the United Kingdom and Europe, leading to acute labour shortages, together with a slower pace of activity in Canada and substantially increased Canadian unemployment, have been largely responsible for a steady decline in both gross and net immigration.

While the pattern of immigration from overseas countries has been characterized by wide swings from year to year, immigration from the United States has grown gradually, almost imperceptibly since the war, from a total of 9,400 in 1947 to 11,516 in 1961. Immigration from the United States appears to have been largely associated with the growth of U.S. ownership and control of Canadian industry.

Over the years, emigration from Canada has largely been motivated by economic reasons. Emigration to the United States has been relatively large and rising, increasing from 32,400 in 1955 to 47,500 in 1961 although a modest decline appears to have occurred in 1962. In addition to native born Canadians, a significant percentage of those emigrating to the United States represent immigrants from Europe who find entry to the United States easier with Canadian citizenship papers. Emigration to overseas countries has become more important in recent years and has increased from 18,400 in 1955 to 25,900 in 1958. On the basis of recent trends it is likely that such emigration has been even greater since 1958. With the general decline in immigration and the over-all increase in emigration, the net gain to Canada has declined substantially since 1957 and disappeared altogether during the latter half of 1961, although a small net increase probably occurred in 1962.

Except for a small deficit in 1950, Canada maintained a moderate surplus position on transactions involving inheritances and migrant funds from 1946 through 1951, owing to a healthy surplus position with the United Kingdom and small surpluses with other overseas countries which were more than enough to offset a deficit position with the United States. Since 1953, however, deficits have been experienced in each year, reaching a high of $79 million in 1960. During the past two years, particularly in 1962, the deficit was reduced substantially (to $39 million in 1962). Since 1949, when Britain placed severe restrictions on the transfer of migrant funds, reducing both the flow of funds and the number of migrants to Canada, the surplus with the United Kingdom has dwindled to marginal proportions. A temporary reversal in 1956 and 1957, producing a surplus of $20 million in the latter year, was quickly wiped out in 1958 when a deficit of $9 million was incurred, the first in the postwar period. During the subsequent three years Canada's position with the United Kingdom has been approximately in balance.

After 1948, Canada experienced significantly heavier immigration from other overseas countries than from the United Kingdom and, since 1950, has earned substantially larger surpluses on transactions with these countries than with the United Kingdom. These surpluses averaged $25 million annually during the years of heavy immigration in the mid-1950s, but since 1957 have declined steadily to $10 million in 1961. The reason is to be found both in a decline in immigration from other overseas countries (from a peak level of 162,000 in 1957 to 48,300 in 1961) and in an increase in emigration to these countries (from 7,800 in 1955 to an estimated 15,000 in 1960).

While only a minor proportion of immigrants to Canada have arrived from the United States, in most years over two thirds of the emigrants leaving Canada have moved to that country. Furthermore, the rate of growth of emigration has been much higher than that for immigration. From 1955 to 1961, for example, emigration from Canada to the United States increased at the rate of over 6 percent per annum while immigration to Canada from the United States grew at an annual rate of less than 2 percent. The disparity in these rates of growth has been reflected in the rapid growth of the deficits which Canada has incurred from the transfer of inheritances and migrant funds between Canada and the United States since the war. For example, the deficit grew from $16 million in 1950 to $91 million in 1960. A reversal in trend occurred in 1961 when the deficit declined to $81 million.

Receipts of inheritances and migrant funds from the United States, which normally have accounted for over 45 percent of the total of such receipts since 1950, have been large in relation to the number of immigrants from that country, especially compared with those derived from immigrants from other lands. In part, this is attributable to the fact that the majority of U.S. immigrants not only come from the highly skilled, managerial or professional classes but also enjoy considerably greater financial resources than even those immigrants from overseas with comparable qualifications.

Another contributing factor may be found in the restrictions imposed by overseas countries upon the conversion of emigrant funds to dollars over much of the postwar period. At times this has served to reduce the amount of funds which immigrants from abroad have been able to bring to Canada in their year of immigration, and has forced them to spread the transfer of such funds to Canada over a period of time. It should also be mentioned that migratory movements between Canada and the United States have probably been marked by the maintenance of close personal and family connections owing to the convenient and relatively inexpensive communications between the two countries. Immigrants from Europe and other overseas countries, on the other hand, because of distance, expense, and lack of time, cannot maintain such close ties with those of their families who have remained at home. Considering these factors and the discrepancies in family wealth, it is most likely that Canadian citizens and residents generally benefit from more numerous and more generous inheritances from their American relatives than they do from their families overseas.

In view of the large net immigration balance which Canada has enjoyed with overseas countries until quite recently, the surplus position on transactions with these countries relating to inheritances and migrant funds has always been relatively small. Receipts have been limited in the past by the factors discussed above and by the more limited financial resources enjoyed by the overseas immigrant compared with his U.S. counterpart. It is worth noting, however, that since 1958 receipts from overseas countries have held fairly steady despite the rapid decline in immigration indicating, perhaps, relaxation of currency controls and the generally higher personal worth of the average immigrant today. The small surpluses, however, are also a reflection of the differential between the financial resources of Canadian emigrants to overseas countries and those of the immigrant to Canada. In other words, although the number of emigrants to overseas countries is small compared with the number of immigrants from these areas, the funds taken out by those emigrants almost match those brought in by a much larger number of immigrants. It would also appear that a larger total amount of inheritances flow to overseas countries from Canada than the reverse.

Canada's receipts of inheritances and migrant funds per immigrant from the United States ($4,348 in 1961) considerably exceed Canada's payments of inheritances and migrant funds per emigrant from Canada to the United States ($2,821 in 1961). This substantial spread has been more than wiped out by the size of Canada's net loss of population to the United States thus accounting for the deficits on transactions with that couutry relating to migrant funds and inheritances.

An encouraging note with respect to overseas emigration and the resulting payment of emigrant funds is the declining trend that has characterized the years 1961 and 1962. The fact that this period was one of expanding economic activity in Canada would appear to have some significance in explaining the reversal in trend. By the same reasoning, however, a period of slack or declining economic activity in Canada, with a continuing high or rising level of unemployment, would appear likely to increase the volume of emigration, with an accompanying increase in payments of emigrant funds. Continuation of the recent declining trend in the deficit on migrant funds will accordingly depend primarily on Canada's ability to provide employment opportunities of a kind and at a rate that bears favourable comparison with that achieved in Europe and the United States.

Over the intermediate term, there is reason to believe that growth rates and employment opportunities in North America will more closely match the European experience than was true over the past five years. Moreover, the opportunities that exist in Canada, as in the United States, for young people to move freely up the educational and income ladders still act as a powerful magnet in attracting immigrants from overseas. Also, in spite of the mis-givings of many, Canadian welfare plans are beginning to equal in com-prehensiveness those in Europe, thus lowering a barrier that in the past has discouraged some emigration from Europe. For many reasons, of which balance of payments is one (but hardly the most important), Canada would benefit from a larger flow of carefully selected immigrants. The record of those who arrived in the mid-1950s reveals that the majority brought needed skills and initiative, created jobs or found steady employment. If current patterns continue it is estimated that net annual immigration of 50,000 or less, if achieved in part by a reduction in net emigration to the United States, would eliminate the deficit from migrant funds and inheritances.

9

Miscellaneous Non-merchandise Transactions

Apart from business services, which have been discussed separately, the miscellaneous category includes official contributions, other types of international government transactions, personal and institutional remittances, and miscellaneous income.

An examination of Canada's net receipts or payments arising from these transactions reveals that, collectively, they have become an increasingly important factor in the balance of payments on non-merchandise transactions. Since 1951, apart from gold production, these miscellaneous items as a group have been the sole contributor of surpluses with the United States. Such transactions with overseas countries, on the other hand, have contributed importantly to Canada's increasing deficit position with these countries. For example, deficits incurred by Canada on such transactions with the United Kingdom, which have exceeded $40 million a year since 1957 and totaled $47 million in 1961, have been of approximately the same size as those resulting from travel expenditures and from interest and dividend payments. With respect to other overseas countries, 80 percent of the total deficit arising from non-merchandise transactions in 1961 arose out of miscellaneous transactions.

Official Contributions and Other Government Transactions

Non-merchandise transactions between the Canadian and other governments fall into two main categories—official contributions and "other government transactions". By and large, official contributions consist of various forms of nonmilitary aid or assistance given by Canada to foreign governments, primarily under the Colombo Plan. Such contributions are mainly an offset to exports to those countries and, therefore, no offsetting receipts appear in the non-merchandise accounts. Except for a small contribution of $3 million to the United Kingdom in 1960, neither that country nor the United States have been recipients of such funds.

In years prior to the establishment of the Colombo Plan in 1952, official contributions primarily represented contributions to the UNRRA and to the International Refugee Organization. In addition, contributions to Palestine and Greece, the UN Korean Relief Agency, the UN International Children's Emergency Fund, and other agencies were also of importance. Since 1952, however, Canada's official contributions have been devoted almost entirely to assistance for less developed countries, particularly India, Ceylon, Malaya, and Pakistan, largely under the Colombo Plan. The increase in official contributions from $16 million in 1952 to $72 million in 1959 was due principally to the latter program of Canadian foreign aid. Since 1957, annual payments under the Colombo Plan have leveled off at roughly $40 million a year and official contributions as a whole declined to $56 million in 1961. Apart from Colombo Plan aid, Canada has continued to make official contributions for the relief of children and refugees and the alleviation of food shortages as they have occurred in different countries.

Government transactions, not accounted for elsewhere, involve payments for defence purposes, the maintenance of diplomatic, trade and other government representations abroad, budgetary contributions to the United Nations and its specialized agencies and to other international Commissions. Other transactions concern the remittance of military and social security pensions abroad, the international transportation of mail and parcels, and acquisition of official property. But they exclude payments for defence imports and exports, as well as mutual aid to NATO countries.

Expenditures on defence constitute the largest element in these government payments. For example, between 1952 and 1960 about one half of Canadian government payments to the United States and the United Kingdom was related to defence activities, as was more than four fifths of payments to the European countries belonging to the Organisation for European Economic Co-operation. Over all, defence spending represented a little under two thirds of total government payments abroad in 1959 and 1960. Since 1952, about 60 percent of these defence expenditures has been made in the OEEC countries to finance contributions to the collective defence forces of NATO. Canada's share has comprised the maintenance in Europe of an army brigade group, an air division, and the provision of financial contributions for the budgets of NATO military headquarters, international staff secretariat, and the common infrastructure programmes. Other military commitments abroad have included Canada's cost of maintaining the UN Emergency Force in the Middle East and of contributing smaller groups of service personnel to truce commissions in Kashmir and Indo-China.

Whereas the United States has been the source of over 80 percent of Canada's receipts in this category (except for 1958 when the proportion was about 75 percent) it has never received more than 28 percent of Canada's payments. Since 1952, Canada has consistently earned surpluses on governmental transactions with the United States. These surpluses were particularly large in 1955 and 1956, when construction of the DEW line in northern Canada was at its peak, and amounted to $139 million and $170 million, respectively. Since 1956, however, they have declined, and in 1961 totaled $54 million.

Canada's contributions to NATO became much more significant following the agreements and decisions reached at the NATO Council Meeting in 1952 at which vastly increased troop commitments were made by the alliance, and the formula for infrastructure cost sharing was determined. These commitments served to raise substantially the size of Canada's payments on government transactions, primarily to overseas countries. In 1953 a $57 million increase in overseas payments principally reflected the purchase of certain supplies and services to discharge Canadian commitments in the Korean War, such services and supplies having been secured from various participants but settled in Canada's account with the United Kingdom. Since 1953, no particular trend has developed either in payments to, or receipts from, overseas countries but such transactions have always been unfavourable to Canada's balance of payments. The resulting deficits have ranged from a low of $60 million in 1954 to a high of $101 million in 1958 and $97 million in 1961, with the United Kingdom usually responsible for around one third, or less, of such deficits.

With the appearance of deficits on government transactions and the increased scale of official contributions in recent years, the combined deficits from these two sources have assumed increasing importance in the over-all deficit position.

TABLE 33

Canadian Non-merchandise Deficits Arising From Official Contributions and Other Government Transactions

(Millions of Dollars)

	1952	1953	1954	1955	1956	1957	1958	1959	1960	1961
With the United States................	+ 88	+105	+ 66	+139	+170	+105	+ 63	+ 82	+ 63	+ 54
With the United Kingdom..............	− 14	− 53	− 19	− 14	− 21	− 28	− 36	− 26	− 25	− 23
With other countries.....	− 39	− 56	− 52	− 88	− 99	−107	−118	−132	−136	−130
Total..............	+ 35	− 4	− 5	+ 37	+ 50	− 30	− 91	− 76	− 98	− 99

It should be pointed out that mutual aid to NATO countries is not included in the foregoing governmental expenditure and, because of the character of military assistance, is not reflected in current balances. Equal amounts are entered in the annual statements of current account with all countries; on the receipts side, to cover the export of goods and services provided as mutual aid; and on the payments side, to represent the contribution. These exports do not appear in totals in regular statistics of Canada's trade with NATO partners, or in the balance of payments statements with individual countries or groups of countries. Between 1950 and 1960 Canada provided $1,650 million in mutual aid to NATO countries, $950 million (nearly 60 percent) of which was dispensed between 1952 and 1955, inclusive, when transfers of equipment from existing service stocks and, to a lesser degree, from new production were heaviest, and when air-crew training in Canada for other NATO countries was at a peak level. With the progressive rearmament of European defence forces and the build-up of their own air-crew training programmes, Canada's contributions in mutual aid tapered off after 1956 to only $43 million in 1960, and in recent years only contributions to infrastructure and NATO budgets have been maintained at earlier levels.

A significant reduction in the deficits Canada incurs from official contributions and government transactions can only be effected by major changes in the country's foreign policy—for example, through decisions to withdraw or reduce commitments to the NATO alliance and to the Colombo Plan, or through a defence agreement with the United States providing for the construction of installations in Canada for the extended use of NORAD or the use of the Strategic Air Command. Only a relatively small reduction in government payments is implied by the recent unilateral decision, in the context of Canada's 1962 balance-of-payments crisis, to reduce Canadian air forces in Europe.

On the other hand, there is a considerable body of opinion in Canada which believes that foreign aid programs should be larger and that Canada should become a member of the Organization of American States. These opinions appear to have some support in various political circles and if translated into policy decisions would, of course, tend to enlarge the deficit on official contributions.

In a political and trading world that is in such an active period of realignment and evolution, the cost in time and money of gaining security, information, and markets is bound to be an increasing one. This is particularly true for Canada in almost all aspects of its external relations. Therefore it would appear realistic to expect government expenditures of the type discussed here to rise rather than decline in the years ahead. But in Canada's circumstances it is important that any such increase in payments should be accompanied by careful consideration of potentials for minimizing their effect on its balance-of-payments position.

Personal and Institutional Remittances

Canada's deficits from personal and institutional remittances grew from $30 million in 1952 to $74 million in 1961, declining to $65 million in 1962.

Personal remittances comprise noncommercial payments between Canadians and residents of other countries. Institutional remittances originate from charitable, religious, and educational organizations. Since 1952, Canada's receipts of such remittances have grown moderately, from $20 million to $26 million in 1962. By far the largest proportion ($19 million in 1961) of these receipts have originated in the United States, reflecting once again the very close personal and cultural links between the two countries. Receipts from all overseas countries have been nominal, never having amounted to more than $6 million a year.

Payments to all countries have grown much faster, from $50 million in 1952 to $98 million in 1961. Payments declined to $91 million in 1962. Payments have been widely distributed, with overseas countries having been the primary beneficiaries, although the proportionate distribution by geographical divisions has been very consistent. For example, the U.S. share of such payments has run between 33 and 38 percent since 1952, that of the United Kingdom from 16 to 20 percent, and that of all other overseas countries from 45 to 48 percent.

TABLE 34

Canadian Non-merchandise Deficits Arising from Personal and Institutional Remittances

(Millions of Dollars)

	1952	1953	1954	1955	1956	1957	1958	1959	1960	1961
With the United States	− 3	− 4	− 5	− 6	− 9	− 10	− 11	− 14	− 14	− 14
With the United Kingdom	− 6	− 7	− 10	− 11	− 12	− 13	− 14	− 16	− 18	− 18
With other countries	− 21	− 22	− 28	− 32	− 35	− 36	− 36	− 41	− 42	− 42
Total	− 30	− 33	− 43	− 49	− 56	− 59	− 61	− 71	− 74	− 74

Heavy immigration in the mid-1950s has certainly been an important element in the growth of personal remittances. Another factor has been the steady advance in wages and the broadly distributed rise in personal incomes and savings. As noted earlier, a large proportion of immigrants arrived from countries other than the United States or the United Kingdom, in which personal incomes generally have been (and continue to be) considerably lower than they are in Canada. There is no doubt, therefore, that a large part of Canada's payments of personal remittances comes from the remittance of funds by new Canadians to people still resident in their former countries. In part, these funds represent repayment of debts incurred in moving to Canada, or remittances to assist relatives and friends to emigrate. Some part of the increase in remittances in 1960 was attributable to the efforts of private groups in Canada in support of the World Refugee Year, striving in particular for refugee camp clearance in Europe and the establishment of vocational training centres for Arab refugees in the Middle East.

Miscellaneous Income

In recent years, around 70 percent of receipts and 85 percent of payments of income on investments appeared in the interest and dividend account. Miscellaneous income, however, includes other transfers of income or profits: such as transfers from branch operations of banks and insurance companies; interest on intercompany loans, mortgages, savings balances, treasury bills, and rentals; and income from the administration of estates, trusts, and agencies. Such transactions have become fairly important in recent years

TABLE 35

Canadian Non-merchandise Deficits
Arising from Transfers of Miscellaneous Income

(Millions of Dollars)

	1952	1953	1954	1955	1956	1957	1958	1959	1960	1961
With the United States.................	− 5	− 5	− 2	− 5	− 9	− 28	− 23	− 19	− 9	− 26
With the United Kingdom..............	− 3	− 2	− 2	− 2	+ 2	− 2	−	− 4	− 6	− 6
With other countries.....	−	+ 2	−	−	− 3	− 8	− 7	− 21	− 27	− 24
Total...............	− 8	− 5	− 4	− 7	− 10	− 38	− 30	− 44	− 42	− 56

between Canada and the United States, but until recently remained insignificant as far as transactions between Canada and overseas countries were concerned. Since 1952, both receipts and payments have almost tripled to a peak figure in 1962 of $102 million for receipts ($82 million in 1961) and of $143 million in 1962 for payments ($138 million in 1961). Since 1954 the deficit has increased from a low in that year of $4 million to a high in 1961 of $56 million. The deficit dropped sharply in 1962 to $41 million. The principal reason was higher interest earnings on credit export sales of wheat and machinery, profits from official transactions in gold, and increased profits of insurance companies.

The U.S. contribution to receipts increased from less than 70 percent in the 1952-56 period to 88 percent in 1961, with the balance roughly divided between the United Kingdom and all other countries. Transferred earnings of financial institutions, principally banks and insurance companies, and, to a lesser extent, investment dealers have been the principal sources of U.S. receipts. The sharp decline in the deficit with the United States in 1960 to $9 million was due largely to extraordinarily large receipts in that year. On the payments side, the United States has been the chief beneficiary.

Until 1955, the U.S. share of such payments remained fairly steady at around 67 percent of the total, or roughly $25 million a year. In that year, however, the level of such payments to the United States began to rise, and by 1961 had reached $98 million. Payments to the United States consist principally of interest on parent-subsidiary company loans, earnings of investment dealers, mutual funds and insurance companies, interest on bank loans and mortgages, and charges for estate and trust administration.

While payments to the United Kingdom have shown little tendency to increase, having fluctuated between $7 million and $11 million each year, payments to other overseas countries began to climb in 1955, and increased from $5 million in 1954 to $31 million in 1960 (23 percent of total payments). As a result, deficits with these countries, which either did not exist or were negligible in previous years, jumped to $27 million in 1960 and $24 million in 1961. Earnings from Canadian mortgage and real estate investments and interest on intercompany loans, and income from securities held through intermediaries for the account of European investors are the principal contributors to increased payments to overseas countries.

In 1960, for all countries, approximately four fifths of these miscellaneous receipts were represented by transfers of profits of financial institutions and an even higher proportion of payments was made up of interest on intercompany borrowings, income from assets managed or administered by trust and loan companies and other financial intermediaries, and profits of insurance companies. The profits of insurance companies for the most part represent transfers of net underwriting profits from branch operations, including earnings on the employment of shareholders' capital and surplus, if any. In some cases, they also cover the provision of services by head office departments. Income from premiums, as well as from reinsurance and claims, is covered in the business services item. International transfers of premiums and claims, however, are not large owing to the practice of insurance companies of investing reserves in the country of risk.

Gold Exports

In balance-of-payments statements, exports and imports of gold are excluded from Canada's trade statistics with the exception of some comparatively small amounts of jewellers' "sweepings" and other industrial forms. Gold production, however, is a source of international credits, and the balance of payments makes provision for it through the item designated nonmonetary gold or "gold production available for export". This item measures the international credits arising from Canadian production, whether the gold is exported and sold abroad or is taken into Canada's official reserves of gold and U.S. dollars. Gold production is taken at the stage which follows refining at the Mint, at which point it can be sold to the Exchange Fund or abroad. Also, it includes sales of commercial gold abroad directly by the producers, as well as gold exported in quartz or ore. In essence, therefore, figures in the current account represent gold production, less gold consumed by industry and the arts, when taken at the final stages of production or refinement.

It is difficult to present transactions involving nonmonetary gold with individual countries. The principal market, however, has been the United States, while the main factor influencing the price of gold has been the official gold purchases of the United States. Furthermore, gold sales to other countries have usually yielded U.S. exchange available for meeting Canada's deficits with the United States. Similarly, that gold production which goes into official reserves is an element shown in capital account with that country. For these reasons, in bilateral statements of Canada's balance of payments, this item is shown exclusively in the current account with the United States.

Gold production available for export has been almost a constant factor over the past decade. Rising from $96 million in 1946 to $163 million in 1950, it has since fluctuated between $144 million and $165 million a year —the latter being the level in 1962.

The prospect of Canada increasing gold production over the intermediate term is not promising unless new high grade gold discoveries are made. International Monetary Fund regulations make it unlikely that the government subsidy for gold production will be increased, while an increase in the price of gold in the near future is unlikely. Gold production available for export, therefore, can be expected to be maintained at approximately the level of recent years.

Statistical Appendix

TABLE 36

Canada's Receipts and Payments on Current Account, 1946-62

(Millions of Dollars)

	1946	1947	1948	1949	1950	1951	1952	1953	1954	1955	1956	1957	1958	1959	1960	1961	1962
Receipts from merchandise exports	2,393	2,723	3,030	2,989	3,139	3,950	4,339	4,152	3,929	4,332	4,837	4,894	4,887	5,150	5,392	5,889	6,364
Receipts from non-merchandise transactions[1]	972	1,025	1,117	1,100	1,101	1,216	1,319	1,339	1,307	1,518	1,627	1,621	1,550	1,642	1,718	1,845	1,984
Payments on merchandise imports	1,822	2,535	2,598	2,696	3,129	4,097	3,850	4,210	3,916	4,543	5,565	5,488	5,066	5,572	5,540	5,716	6,209
Payments on non-merchandise transactions[1]	1,180	1,164	1,098	1,216	1,445	1,586	1,644	1,724	1,752	2,005	2,265	2,482	2,502	2,724	2,813	3,000	2,987
Balance on merchandise trade	+571	+188	+432	+293	+ 10	−147	+489	− 58	+ 13	−211	− 728	− 594	− 179	− 422	− 148	+ 173	+ 155
Balance on non-merchandise transactions	−208	−139	+ 19	−116	−344	−370	−325	−385	−445	−487	− 638	− 861	− 952	−1,082	−1,095	−1,155	−1,003
Current account balance	+363	+ 49	+451	+177	−334	−517	+164	−443	−432	−698	−1,366	−1,455	−1,131	−1,504	−1,243	− 982	− 848

[1] Excludes Mutual Aid to NATO countries.

TABLE 37

Deficits and Surpluses in Canada's Non-merchandise Transactions, 1946-61

(Millions of Dollars)

Category / Country	1946	1947	1948	1949	1950	1951	1952	1953	1954	1955	1956	1957	1958	1959	1960	1961
Travel expenditures																
U.S.	+86	+89	+154	+102	+67	+12	-37	-25	-37	-60	-82	-78	-104	-97	-87	-24
U.K.	—	-2	-3	-6	-12	-12	-17	-19	-22	-27	-32	-29	-34	-44	-50	-50
Other	—	-3	-6	-4	-6	-6	-12	-19	-25	-34	-47	-55	-55	-66	-70	-86
Total	+86	+84	+145	+92	+49	-6	-66	-63	-84	-121	-161	-162	-193	-207	-207	-160
Interest and dividends																
U.S.	-203	-238	-230	-285	-361	-325	-259	-233	-276	-310	-347	-385	-400	-448	-429	-533
U.K.	-47	-45	-41	-46	-48	-27	-27	-29	-27	-34	-59	-68	-68	-55	-51	-52
Other	+8	+10	+16	+24	+25	+17	+18	+23	+27	+21	+25	+18	+24	+14	—	+24
Total	-242	-273	-255	-307	-384	-335	-268	-239	-276	-323	-381	-435	-444	-489	-480	-561
Freight and shipping																
U.S.	-68	-117	-82	-67	-83	-112	-128	-132	-92	-84	-128	-129	-88	-98	-104	-103
U.K.	+75	+82	+71	+57	+25	+48	+63	+37	+34	+48	+39	+26	+14	+5	+4	+7
Other	+85	+79	+68	+60	+41	+61	+73	+39	+15	+19	+44	+33	+15	+2	+9	+14
Total	+92	+44	+57	+50	-17	-3	+8	-56	-43	-17	-45	-70	-59	-91	-91	-82
Inheritances and migrant funds																
U.S.	-12	-19	-19	-26	-16	-23	-39	-33	-33	-37	-49	-77	-57	—	+1	+59
U.K.	+42	+39	+45	+28	+10	+4	+8	+6	+6	+4	+10	+20	+9	+15	+11	+2
Other	—	—	+8	+7	+10	+26	+40	+54	+32	+52	+55	+90	+96	+56	+79	+10
Total	+30	+20	+34	+9	+4	+7	+9	+27	+5	+19	+16	+33	+48	+71	+91	+71
Gold production																
Total	+96	+99	+119	+139	+163	+150	+150	+144	+155	+155	+150	+147	+160	+148	+162	+162
Business services and other transactions																
U.S.	n.a.	n.a.	n.a.	n.a.	n.a.	n.a.	-145	-133	-138	-142	-168	-177	-181	-177	-179	-204
U.K.	n.a.	n.a.	n.a.	n.a.	n.a.	n.a.	+7	+7	+2	+1	+1	+2	+3	+5	+2	+4
Other	n.a.	n.a.	n.a.	n.a.	n.a.	n.a.	+1	-3	-4	-2	-2	-6	-8	-10	-9	-14
Total	-42	n.a.	n.a.	n.a.	-138	-165	-137	-129	-140	-143	-169	-181	-186	-182	-186	-214
All other miscellaneous																
U.S.	n.a.	n.a.	n.a.	n.a.	n.a.	n.a.	+80	+96	+59	+128	+152	+67	+29	+49	+40	+14
U.K.	n.a.	n.a.	n.a.	n.a.	n.a.	n.a.	+23	+62	+31	+27	+31	+43	+50	+46	+49	+47
Other	n.a.	n.a.	n.a.	n.a.	n.a.	n.a.	-100	+4	+80	+120	+137	+151	+161	+194	+205	+196
Total	-28	n.a.	n.a.	-13	-13	+18	+3	+42	+52	-19	+16	-127	-182	-191	-214	-229
Total																
U.S.	-177	-244	-104	-223	-353	-435	-378	-316	-362	-350	-472	-632	-641	-694	-688	-771
U.K.	+12	+66	+70	+45	+46	+4	+11	-60	-40	-36	-73	-96	-125	-150	-147	-144
Other	-43	+39	+53	+62	-37	+61	+42	-9	-43	-101	-93	-133	-186	-238	-260	-240
Total	-208	-139	+19	-116	-344	-370	-325	-385	-445	-487	-638	-861	-952	-1,082	-1,095	-1,155

n.a. Not available.

TABLE 38
Canada's Total Non-merchandise Transactions with the United States and Overseas Countries, 1946-62[1]
(Millions of Dollars)

Year	With the United States			With Overseas Countries			With All Countries		
	Receipts	Payments	Balance	Receipts	Payments	Balance	Receipts	Payments	Balance
1946	619	796	−177	353	384	− 31	972	1,180	− 208
1947	651	895	−244	374	269	+105	1,025	1,164	− 139
1948	739	843	−104	378	255	+123	1,117	1,098	+ 19
1949	748	971	−223	352	245	+107	1,100	1,216	− 116
1950	831	1,184	−353	270	261	+ 9	1,101	1,445	− 344
1951	852	1,287	−435	364	299	+ 65	1,216	1,586	− 370
1952	928	1,306	−378	391	338	+ 53	1,319	1,644	− 325
1953	985	1,301	−316	354	423	− 69	1,339	1,724	− 385
1954	951	1,313	−362	356	439	− 83	1,307	1,752	− 445
1955	1,102	1,452	−350	416	553	−137	1,518	2,005	− 487
1956	1,161	1,633	−472	466	632	−166	1,627	2,265	− 638
1957	1,139	1,771	−632	482	711	−229	1,621	2,482	− 861
1958	1,102	1,743	−641	448	759	−311	1,550	2,502	− 952
1959	1,189	1,883	−694	453	841	−388	1,642	2,724	−1,082
1960	1,239	1,927	−688	479	886	−407	1,718	2,813	−1,095
1961	1,297	2,068	−771	552	936	−384	1,845	3,000	−1,155
1962	1,441	2,082	−641	543	905	−362	1,984	2,987	−1,003

[1] Excluding Mutual Aid to NATO Countries.

TABLE 39
Travel Expenditures Between Canada and the United States and Other Countries, 1946-62
(Millions of Dollars)

Year	With the United States			With Overseas Countries			With All Countries		
	Receipts	Payments	Balance	Receipts	Payments	Balance	Receipts	Payments	Balance
1946	216	130	+ 86	5	5	0	221	135	+ 86
1947	241	152	+ 89	10	15	− 5	251	167	+ 84
1948	267	113	+154	12	21	− 9	279	134	+145
1949	267	165	+102	18	28	− 10	285	193	+ 92
1950	260	193	+ 67	15	33	− 18	275	226	+ 49
1951	258	246	+ 12	16	34	− 18	274	280	− 6
1952	257	294	− 37	18	47	− 29	275	341	− 66
1953	282	307	− 25	20	58	− 38	302	365	− 63
1954	283	320	− 37	22	69	− 47	305	389	− 84
1955	303	363	− 60	25	86	− 61	328	449	−121
1956	309	391	− 82	28	107	− 79	337	498	−161
1957	325	403	− 78	38	122	− 84	363	525	−162
1958	309	413	−104	40	129	− 89	349	542	−193
1959	351	448	− 97	40	150	−110	391	598	−207
1960	375	462	− 87	45	165	−120	420	627	−207
1961	435	459	− 24	47	183	−136	482	642	−160
1962	510	420	+ 90	50	190	−140	560	610	− 50

TABLE 40
Interest and Dividend Transactions Between Canada and the United States and Other Countries, 1946-62
(Millions of Dollars)

Year	With the United States			With Overseas Countries			With All Countries		
	Receipts	Payments	Balance	Receipts	Payments	Balance	Receipts	Payments	Balance
1946	47	250	−203	23	62	−39	70	312	−242
1947	36	274	−238	28	63	−35	64	337	−273
1948	37	267	−230	33	58	−25	70	325	−255
1949	40	325	−285	43	65	−22	83	390	−307
1950	50	411	−361	41	64	−23	91	475	−384
1951	57	382	−325	58	68	−10	115	450	−335
1952	85	344	−259	60	69	− 9	145	413	−268
1953	101	334	−233	64	70	− 6	165	404	−239
1954	69	345	−276	78	78	0	147	423	−276
1955	78	388	−310	82	95	−13	160	483	−323
1956	80	427	−347	62	96	−34	142	523	−381
1957	95	480	−385	59	109	−50	154	589	−435
1958	100	500	−400	68	112	−44	168	612	−444
1959	99	547	−448	83	124	−41	182	671	−489
1960	102	531	−429	71	122	−51	173	653	−480
1961	109	642	−533	100	128	−28	209	770	−561
1962	n.a.	n.a.	n.a.	n.a.	n.a.	n.a.	211	781	−570

n.a. Not available.

TABLE 41

Business Services and Other Transactions Between Canada and the United States and Other Countries, 1952-62

(Millions of Dollars)

Year	With the United States			With Overseas Countries			With All Countries		
	Receipts	Payments	Balance	Receipts	Payments	Balance	Receipts	Payments	Balance
1952........	79	224	−145	29	21	+ 8	108	245	−137
1953........	87	220	−133	31	27	+ 4	118	247	−129
1954........	95	233	−138	30	32	− 2	125	265	−140
1955........	103	245	−142	34	35	− 1	137	280	−143
1956........	107	275	−168	39	40	− 1	146	315	−166
1957........	109	286	−177	40	44	− 4	149	330	−181
1958........	112	293	−181	45	50	− 5	157	343	−186
1959........	120	297	−177	46	51	− 5	166	348	−182
1960........	127	306	−179	52	59	− 7	179	365	−186
1961........	129	333	−204	56	66	−10	185	399	−214
1962........	n.a.	n.a.	n.a.	n.a.	n.a.	n.a.	184	430	−246

n.a. Not available.

TABLE 42

Freight and Shipping Transactions Between Canada and the United States and Other Countries, 1946-62

(Millions of Dollars)

Year	With the United States			With Overseas Countries			With All Countries		
	Receipts	Payments	Balance	Receipts	Payments	Balance	Receipts	Payments	Balance
1946........	101	169	− 68	210	50	+160	311	219	+ 92
1947........	104	221	−117	218	57	+161	322	278	+ 44
1948........	131	213	− 82	205	66	+139	336	279	+ 57
1949........	126	193	− 67	177	60	+117	303	253	+ 50
1950........	157	240	− 83	127	61	+ 66	284	301	− 17
1951........	164	276	−112	187	78	+109	351	354	− 3
1952........	174	302	−128	209	73	+136	383	375	+ 8
1953........	164	296	−132	154	78	+ 76	318	374	− 56
1954........	169	261	− 92	144	95	+ 49	313	356	− 43
1955........	203	287	− 84	195	128	+ 67	398	415	− 17
1956........	223	351	−128	234	151	+ 83	457	502	− 45
1957........	222	351	−129	223	164	+ 59	445	515	− 70
1958........	206	294	− 88	195	166	+ 29	401	460	− 59
1959........	228	326	− 98	192	199	− 7	420	525	−105
1960........	220	324	−104	222	209	+ 13	442	533	− 91
1961........	230	333	−103	256	235	+ 21	486	568	− 82
1962........	n.a.	n.a.	n.a.	n.a.	n.a.	n.a.	498	588	− 90

n.a. Not available.

TABLE 43

Transactions in Inheritances and Migrant Funds Between Canada and the United States and Other Countries, 1946-62

(Millions of Dollars)

Year	With the United States			With Overseas Countries			With All Countries		
	Receipts	Payments	Balance	Receipts	Payments	Balance	Receipts	Payments	Balance
1946........	19	31	−12	46	4	+42	65	35	+30
1947........	18	37	−19	51	12	+39	69	49	+20
1948........	18	37	−19	66	13	+53	84	50	+ 34
1949........	18	44	−26	50	15	+35	68	59	+ 9
1950........	31	47	−16	26	14	+12	57	61	− 4
1951........	32	55	−23	45	15	+30	77	70	+ 7
1952........	38	77	−39	47	17	+30	85	94	− 9
1953........	41	74	−33	50	17	+33	91	91	0
1954........	42	75	−33	47	19	+28	89	94	− 5
1955........	45	82	−37	41	23	+18	86	105	−19
1956........	45	94	−49	54	21	+33	99	115	−16
1957........	47	124	−77	77	33	+44	124	157	−33
1958........	47	104	−57	50	41	+ 9	97	145	−48
1959........	52	123	−71	57	42	+15	109	165	−56
1960........	50	141	−91	52	40	+12	102	181	−79
1961........	51	134	−83	52	40	+12	103	174	−71
1962........	n.a.	n.a.	n.a.	n.a.	n.a.	n.a.	124	163	−39

n.a. Not available.

75

TABLE 44

Miscellaneous Non-merchandise Transactions Between Canada and the United States and Other Countries, 1952-62

(Millions of Dollars)

Year	With the United States			With Overseas Countries			With All Countries		
	Receipts	Payments	Balance	Receipts	Payments	Balance	Receipts	Payments	Balance
1952	145	65	+ 80	28	111	− 83	173	176	− 3
1953	166	70	+ 96	35	173	−138	201	243	− 42
1954	138	79	+ 59	35	146	−111	173	225	− 52
1955	215	87	+128	39	186	−147	254	273	− 19
1956	247	95	+152	49	217	−168	296	312	− 16
1957	194	127	+ 67	45	239	−194	239	366	−127
1958	168	139	+ 29	50	261	−211	218	400	−182
1959	191	142	+ 49	35	275	−240	226	417	−191
1960	203	163	+ 40	37	291	−254	240	454	−214
1961	181	167	+ 14	37	280	−243	240	447	−229
1962	n.a.	n.a.	n.a.	n.a.	n.a.	n.a.	242	415	−173

n.a. Not available.

Canadian-American Committee Members

Co-chairmen

ROBERT M. FOWLER
  President, Canadian Pulp & Paper Association, Montreal, Que.

R. DOUGLAS STUART
  Director, The Quaker Oats Company, Chicago, Ill.

Members

WILLIAM L. BATT
  Delray Beach, Fla.

T. N. BEAUPRÉ
  President, British Columbia Forest Products Limited, Vancouver, B.C.

J A. BEIRNE
  President, Communications Workers of America, AFL-CIO, Washington, D.C.

RALPH P. BELL
  Honorary Director, Bank of Nova Scotia, Halifax, Nova Scotia

L. J. BELNAP
  Chairman, Consolidated Paper Corporation, Ltd., Montreal, Que.

HAROLD BOESCHENSTEIN
  President, Owens-Corning Fiberglas Corporation, Toledo, Ohio

GEORGE BURT
  Director, Region No. 7, United Automobile, Aircraft, and Agricultural Implement Workers of America, AFL-CIO-CLC, Windsor, Ont.

EARL L. BUTZ
  Dean, School of Agriculture, Agricultural Experiment Station, Purdue University, Lafayette, Ind.

MARCEL FARIBAULT
  President and General Manager, General Trust of Canada, Montreal, Que.

HAROLD S. FOLEY
  Vancouver, B.C.

DONALD GORDON
  Chairman and President, Canadian National Railways, Montreal, Que.

H. H. HANNAM
  President and Managing Director, The Canadian Federation of Agriculture, Ottawa, Ont.

F. PEAVEY HEFFELFINGER
  Chairman of the Board, F. H. Peavey & Company, Minneapolis, Minn.

CHARLES L. HUSTON, JR.
  President, Lukens Steel Company, Coatesville, Pa.

CURTIS M. HUTCHINS
  President, St. Croix Paper Company, New York, N.Y.

CLAUDE JODOIN
  President, Canadian Labour Congress, Ottawa, Ont.

VERNON E. JOHNSON
  Chairman of the Board, Canadian International Paper Company, Montreal, Que.

JOSEPH D. KEENAN
  International Secretary, International Brotherhood of Electrical Workers, AFL-CIO, Washington, D.C.

CHARLES H. KELLSTADT
  Chairman of the Board, Sears, Roebuck & Company, Chicago, Ill.

W. S. KIRKPATRICK
  President, The Consolidated Mining & Smelting Company of Canada Limited, Montreal, Que.

R. A. LAIDLAW
  Secretary and Director, R. Laidlaw Lumber Company, Ltd., Toronto, Ont.

MAURICE LAMONTAGNE
  Ottawa, Ont.

HERBERT H. LANK
  President, Du Pont of Canada Limited, Montreal, Que.

DONALD MacDONALD
  Secretary-Treasurer, Canadian Labour Congress, Ottawa, Ont.